THE HOUSE THAT
CHRIST
BUILT

DR. ARIETTA S. GRIMMETT

THE HOUSE THAT
CHRIST
BUILT

AT THE COST OF HIS BLOOD

Julia, you are such a dear friend. I appreciate you for who you are.

Arietta Grimmett.

TATE PUBLISHING
AND ENTERPRISES, LLC

Published by Tate Publishing & Enterprises, LLC
127 E. Trade Center Terrace | Mustang, Oklahoma 73064 USA
1.888.361.9473 | www.tatepublishing.com

Tate Publishing is committed to excellence in the publishing industry. The company reflects the philosophy established by the founders, based on Psalm 68:11,
"The Lord gave the word and great was the company of those who published it."

Book design copyright © 2016 by Tate Publishing, LLC. All rights reserved.
Cover design by Norlan Balazo
Interior design by Jomar Ouano

Published in the United States of America

ISBN: 978-1-68319-288-6
1. Religion / Christian Church / General
2. Religion / Christian Life / Personal Growth
16.06.03

To the family of God.

*So then, you are no longer foreigners and strangers. On
the contrary, you are fellow-citizens with God's people
and members of God's family. You have been built on
the foundation of the emissaries and the prophets, with
the cornerstone being Yeshua the Messiah himself. In
union with him the whole building is held together
and it is growing into a holy temple in union with the
Lord. Yes, in union with him you yourselves are being
built together into a spiritual dwelling-place for God.*

—Ephesians 2:19–22, cjb

*He will be the stability of your times, a wealth
of salvation, wisdom and knowledge, and fear of
ADONAI, which is his treasure.*

—Isaiah 33:6, cjb

Acknowledgements

First and foremost, I thank Jesus for helping me write this book. It truly was an honor and I felt at times so unworthy.

I thank my boss, Donna Payton, at Helping Hands of Cleveland for allowing me to take time off to spend an enormous amount of time writing this book and then taking me back after my completion of the book with the exception of a few changes.

I thank my children—Cynthia, Sherleen, and William (BJ)—and their families for their understanding when I moved back to Cleveland, Tennessee; a time that I was to be by myself to concentrate on writing. It has been very hard without my family.

I thank every pastor in my life that was instrumental in my spiritual growth. Pastors Doug Bell, Foster Bell, Jimmie Bentley, Albert Chatmon Sr., Richard Clark, Sam Clements, Lettie Hebert, Sandy Meador, William Norton, Van Sullivan, Brian Sutton, and Bobby Tager.

I thank the overseers who were instrumental in my spiritual growth: Bishop Robin Balram, Bishop Albert Chatmon Sr., and Bishop Leroy Greenaway.

I thank those who encouraged me along the way: Linda Bowman, Jean Campbell, Reta Dawson, Edsel Hartman, Kay and Perry Horner, Elva Howard, Linda Humberd, Jeanette Rollins, and Dr. Mattie Wade.

Contents

Forethought

Much heaviness is on my heart as I think about the ravenous wolves who have tried to destroy something so beautiful—the house that Christ built. I have seen those who have been hurt, misled, ignored, and downright degraded because they did not believe the same way.

I have felt for some time that time is running out for God's family to get it together. He is coming again; and He is coming for His children. "For the Lord himself will come down from heaven with a rousing cry, with a call from one of the ruling angels, and with God's shofar; those who died united with the Messiah will be the first to rise; then we who are left still alive will be caught up with them in the clouds to meet the Lord in the air; and thus we will always be with the Lord" (1 Thessalonians 4:16, 17, cjb).

As a body of people, a holy nation, a peculiar (special) people, we have to be ready for His return. This book is to encourage you as a Believer in Christ to understand that His Word reveals that He is coming after His family, His children, people who have accepted Jesus Christ as their Lord and Savior. He is coming after all who believe that He is who He says He is: King of kings and Lord of lords.

As you read this book, take into account that His family is scattered throughout this earth; but by His Spirit we are one in Him. With this understanding, let us begin our journey of watching Christ the Messiah build His house.

Suppose one of you wants to build a tower. Don't you sit down and estimate the cost, to see if you have enough capital to complete it? If you don't, then when you have laid the foundation but can't finish, all the onlookers start making fun of you and say, "This is the man who began to build, but couldn't finish."

—Luke 14:28, CJB

Introduction

Have you ever wanted to know where you came from; where your ancestors originated from a few generations back? I have and I am sure many of you have as well. Ancestry. com is used quite extensively by those who have a desire to know their ancestors and are always looking for a leaf that will reveal someone they did not know about. Is it safe to say that you also want to know your roots?

Personally, I am like many of you; and I found information that I was not aware of. In the process, it turns out that my forefathers came from England, Ireland, Germany, and here in these United States American Indians. When I was searching out my ancestry, I also found out that my grandfather's name, five generations back, was Abraham; and, of course, that started me thinking about my spiritual heritage. However, it took me a lot longer to figure out that I too was connected to Abraham, the biblical patriarch, and Sarah just as all of God's children is.

The song lyrics, "Father Abraham had many sons (daughters); and many sons have Father Abraham; and I am one of them and so are you; so let's just praise the Lord," didn't have real meaning to me until I realized that through Christ I am a part of Abraham's seed. When we look at Abraham's seed, we understand it as being his physical seed, but it also can be seen as those of Abraham's seed, the Jewish people, who are genuine believers living by faith. Also Abraham's seed refers to all Gentiles who have accepted Jesus Christ as their personal savior. Therefore, as Gentile Christians, it simply means that we are "heirs of the promise given to all the families of the earth" through the new covenant that was referred to in Jeremiah 31:31–34, CJB. The seed of Abraham that is being referred to, is Jesus Christ.

I will be quoting quite a few Scriptures, and I will be taking them from the Complete Jewish Bible (CJB) throughout my book. There will be a few instances where I will use the KJV. My simple explanation for using the CJB is that this Bible was written by a Jewish believer; and he has given a tremendous insight into the original Hebrew writings. I will give more information on the writer of the CJB later. With this understanding, let us begin to unfold the mystery through His Word that God wants to reveal to His children.

I will lay the groundwork by beginning in Genesis 18: 19, CJB: "For I have made myself known to him, so that he will give orders to his children and to his household after him to keep the way of *ADONAI* and to do what is right and just, so that *ADONAI* may bring about for Avraham (Abraham) what he has promised him." Also, Genesis 12:3, cjb: "I will bless those who bless you, but I will curse anyone who curses you; and by you all the families of the earth will be blessed." Gentiles will be blessed through the coming Messiah when He is accepted as their Lord and Savior through the new covenant. The new covenant is first mentioned by the prophet Jeremiah.

> "Here, the days are coming," says *ADONAI*, "when I will make a new covenant with the house of Isra'el and with the house of Y'hudah. It will not be like the covenant I made with their fathers on the day I took them by their hand and brought them out of the land of Egypt; because they, for their part, violated my covenant, even though I, for my part, was a husband to them," says *ADONAI*. "For this is the covenant I will make with the house of Isra'el after those days," says *ADONAI*. "I will put my *Torah* (laws) within them and write it on their hearts; I will be their God, and they will be my people. No longer will any of them teach his fellow community member or his brother, 'Know *ADONAI*'; for all will know me, from the least of them to the greatest; because I will forgive their wickednesses and remember their sins no more."

> Jeremiah 31:30–33, cjb)

You will see how the above Scriptures will unfold and how they are related to the house that Christ built. I am going to get some of the misconceptions out of the way before we go any further. There are Christian organizations that believe with all their heart that they are the chosen ones that will be the Bride of Christ; and those outside their faith will be guests at the Marriage Supper of the Lamb. When I was teaching a course on eschatology from the book *Understanding End Times Prophecy* at Faith Christian University and Schools in Maryland a few years ago, and after extensive study, I understand many scriptures differently concerning what is known today as the church or the body of Christ.

Let us continue. There are those who believe it was Christ who built the church on Peter and the way into heaven is accomplished by works. There are those who believe that the church started on the Day of Pentecost when the Holy Ghost fell on the 120 who were present in the upper room. We also know there are other folks who use the Koran, or a book written by John Smith, or the Jehovah's Witness book as their authoritative Word of God. Paul stated in Galatians 1:7 (CJB) that there would be those who will be "pestering you and trying to pervert the genuine Good News of the Messiah."

I will not delve into these problems, because the truths of God's Word will reveal to His family what is truth. My emphasis will be on Jesus Christ and Him crucified, His family, and the house that Christ built, and how His house is still standing today.

However, I must mention that there are those who also believe that what we call the church has replaced Israel. This particular belief is known as replacement theology. I will discuss this topic briefly. But you must remember from reading the New Testament that many of God's children had misconceptions about truth; that is why Christ trained twelve to carry on with His truths.

Let us get back to replacement theology and its fallacy. God's covenant with Abraham and His seed was a perpetual covenant, never to be forgotten.[1] The above scripture, Jeremiah 31:30–33, is referring to the time of Moses and the Mosaic covenant or law and how they could not live up to the law. Therefore, a new covenant was going to be established. As mentioned in the verses above, "I will put my Torah within them and write it on their hearts, I will be their God, and they will be my people." He was referring to the descendants of His people under covenant, the seed of Abraham, Isaac, and Jacob, that they (Abraham's descendants) would receive a new covenant. This did not diminish the perpetual covenant that God made with

---

1 The Webster Dictionary defines perpetual as "continuous, lasting or enduring forever continuing indefinitely without interruption; unceasing."

Abraham, Isaac, and Jacob. The new covenant was actually an addition or an addendum, if you please, to the original Covenant; and is referring to Jesus Christ, the seed that "would bruise Satan's head." The new covenant is too a perpetual covenant that God has made for His children to have access to His throne room.

The prophecy regarding the new covenant is referring to all who will receive the Messiah Jesus Christ as their personal Savior as brought out in Genesis 12:3b, "By you all the families of the earth will be blessed." This of course included the Gentiles. The Jewish people have contributed to all the families of the earth from the first polio vaccine, to arts, music, and even to creating Hershey's chocolate and the most beautiful blessing of all, the Son of God: the Messiah.

The only way that the laws of God can be written on anyone's heart, Jew or Gentile, is through Christ Jesus. He shed His blood and sealed the new covenant as perpetual not only for the Gentiles but also for His very own, the Jewish people. Isaiah prophesies of Israel's redemption. (See chapters 48, 49, cjb) A quote from Isaiah 49:16 was referring to His chosen people—Israel, "I have engraved you on the palms of my hands, your walls are always before me." Also read Romans chapters 10 and 11. Israel has not been forgotten or forsaken. Actually, God's Old Testament children literally lived by faith in the coming Messiah. We know this by reading Hebrews chapter 11. All of those who believe in Jesus Christ as the Savior of the world from the beginning to the end must live by faith in Him.

What we refer to as the Mosaic covenant or law was given to the children of Israel to reveal to them God's righteousness, judgments, and ordinances. The Mosaic covenant was conditional; whereas, the Abrahamic covenant is unconditional. The Ten Commandments or Mosaic covenant were given to His children to reveal that they were a very sinful people, but it was impossible for the commandments to save them, only their faith in the coming Messiah could save them. This proved to be true because of their continuous rebellious spirit throughout the wonderings in the wilderness and generations after their deliverance. It was not until Christ came that a divine nature could actually be imputed into man which bears witness of the new covenant. "I will put my Torah or my laws within them and write it on their hearts." This comes about by asking Jesus Christ to become your personal Savior by repenting of your sins, and believing by faith that He has the power and authority to forgive you.

With this understanding, we are about to embark on a journey to come to know and understand our spiritual heritage as, if you were like me, never before understood. Stick with me and enjoy the ride. It may get bumpy, but I ask you to hang in there and allow the Holy Ghost speak to you as you read and determine for yourself if this ancestry is yours also.

He is like someone building a house who dug deep and laid the foundation on bedrock. When a flood came, the torrent beat against that house but couldn't shake it, because it was constructed well.

—Luke 6:48, CJB

1

Firstborn Son

As we are aware, the first house that Christ built was man. This was God's plan from the foundation of the world. He did not build man because He was lonely. Yes, there was/ is one God but we must remember, He wasn't alone; in the godhead there are three—Father, Son, and Holy Ghost. Can we truthfully even say that in the beginning God was ever alone? But we surely can say, "He was never lonely." We are mere dirt, clay, dust, if you please, why would God need us in order not to be lonely. Even if you wanted to call Him lonely; remember, He had a host of angels worshiping Him at all times. No, God was not lonely although the angels were made to worship him and to be ministering spirits. He was God all by Himself; therefore, He truly doesn't need anyone to satisfy loneliness, for one simple reason: He is all sufficient within Himself. I can accept that God created us to have a family; a family who would desire to worship and love Him simply for who He is—Creator God. And a family He could love and care for in return. From reading His Word, He is truly a relational God. We know this by the Trinity, the host of angels and His desire to build a man and a woman.

With that being said, let us continue. Since God is omniscient, He knew that his first house, Adam, would fall. Why do I call Adam God's first house? Adam laid on that ground, after being formed, as a hunk of dirt, or not to be offensive to some, a hunk of clay, with no life in him; but then God, I would like to think, cradled him in His arms and breathed the breath of life into him. Then and only then did man become a living soul. The body of the man was a house built for that living soul that God breathed into him. He was not a being or a living soul prior to the breath of God entering his body. Man is spirit, and if he had not received that breath of life after he was wholly built, he would not have existed. He would have been just a hunk of clay—a form without life lying in the dirt. Also, the first man Adam (spirit and soul) is housed in flesh (body) in order to accomplish God's purpose for him, not only to procreate but also to remain in His own image. Therefore, God created or built a body and all the intricate parts of the body, including heart, lungs, veins, etc. around man's spirit and then breathed the breath of life into him, to become a living soul. We are definitely "fearfully and wonderfully made." We too are trinity—body, soul, and spirit.

When we became a living soul, our spirit received a conscience awareness of our being which is housed in our body. Our conscience awareness motivates our mind, will, and emotions. God is Spirit and He too has a conscience awareness of who He is. The great I AM that I AM: all-sufficient, in need of nothing or no one but Himself. And He created us to need Him.

Not only was the outer shell of man created to house his spirit, his complete being was built to house his soul, the very breath of God. The question I ask you is, "How important is it for you to know your Creator?" I will answer that question with a question, "How important is it for you to breath?" This road that you are about to continue on will take you to an intimate place where you can encounter a very personal God who already knows you personally; actually knew you even before you were formed in your mother's womb.

Now that we have established that the first house Christ built was man, we will move on to what happened to that house. But even before we do that, we also have to establish that it was Christ who built the first house. "In the beginning was the Word, and the Word was with God, and the Word was God. He was with God in the beginning. All things came to be through him, and without him nothing made had being. In him was life, and the life was the light of mankind" (John 1:1–4, cjb). The very life that was breathed into Adam was light. Light to understand who God was when He walked with Adam and Eve in the cool of the day in the garden of Eden. "God is light, and there is no darkness in him—none" (1 John 1:5b, cjb).

In other words, the Son of God was there in the beginning and actually man was made by Him. "All things came to be through him, and without him nothing made had being." The house that Christ built has begun. With blueprint in hand, building begins; and it will be constructed according to His plans.

To sum the first house up: Man was made with a spirit, body, and soul. Man is spirit housed in flesh, and with the breath of God became a living soul. Only a unique person could perform such a miracle and His name is God, but yet we will come to know Him as Savior, Redeemer, Lord and Master—Jesus Christ, the Son of the living God, the Messiah.[1]

---

1 How can we, as mere mortals, distinguish between God the Father, God the Son and God the Holy Ghost? Many can't comprehend that there is one God but yet three persons. No one can fully understand this fact with a carnal mind. But with a spiritual mind, we come to understand that the Son is the express essence of His Father; and the Holy Spirit is the express image of the Father and the Son; thus three persons or beings but one God.

Because of Adam's disobedience, the first house that Christ built fell; therefore, God's intended family would be totally separated from their Creator. We will look into what happened to the first man Adam. Keep in mind "first man Adam"; it is very important to remember that he was created in the image and likeness of God.

The serpent said to the woman,
"It is not true that you will surely die."

—Genesis 3:4, CJB

2

What Happened to the House that Christ Built?

The answer to that question is very simple—man disobeyed God; therefore the house that Christ built fell. A house whose foundation is ignored will fall. It will not do any good to keep it clean and in good shape on the inside if the very foundation is not taken care of. When man succumbed to the temptation of Satan, he needed an overhaul, for lack of a better word; or we could say a *do-over* from the inside out, starting with the foundation. God had built man with a solid foundation in His own image, but His image had been tainted with sin.

To start God's family, I also must establish that when God built Adam, He also built a woman (man with a womb) and took her to Adam to be his helpmeet. God called them both Adam. Adam named his wife "Eve because she was the mother of all living." God saw them both as one, equal if you please. At that time, the only difference was Eve had a womb to carry Adam's seed. They were to procreate; in other words, add to the family of God. The garden of Eden was not meant just for Adam and Eve; they were to have sons and daughters.

The garden of Eden, I believe, was the first spiritual house of God for man to dwell in. This was where God walked with them in the cool of the day. He would not have visited that garden if it were not pure. In that garden, He planted trees that were pleasant to the eyes to look at; and also good to eat. And in the midst of the garden, God planted the tree of life; but with a prohibition, He planted the tree of knowledge of good and evil. Do not eat from the tree of knowledge of good and evil. "*ADONAI*, God, gave the person this order: 'You may freely eat from every tree in the garden except the tree of the knowledge of good and evil. You are not to eat from it, because on the day that you eat from it, it will become certain that you will die'" (Genesis 2:16, 17, CJB).

God intended Adam and Eve to live forever both spiritually and physically in His image and likeness: perfect. Like God, they too could think, process their thoughts, and act on their thoughts. But because of their disobedience, they were forced from the garden to live because the garden was created for a perfect people—a perfect family. After they ate from the tree of knowledge of good and evil, they were made to leave the garden. God also guarded the garden from them by placing cherubim and a flaming sword which turned every way to protect the tree of life from them. (See Genesis 3:24, CJB)

Adam and Eve now knew good and evil. The good was obedience and evil was disobedience. They knew what good was because prior to knowing evil they walked and talked with their Creator and they were not ashamed of their nakedness. They too now understood evil because of their disobedience and feeling the shame of it. Because their eyes were opened to understand the difference between good and evil they, for the first time, felt shame; the shame of their nakedness. Even though they had become like God when they ate from the tree of knowledge of good and evil, they would suffer the consequence as well as all mankind. From that day forward all mankind would be born with a sinful human nature. They were like God because God knew what evil would do to a person as well as what good would do. God was all good but He knew evil and the repercussions of it. God had dealt with evil in heaven when He cast out Lucifer and his angels. And too, after sinning, Adam and Eve knew both good and evil.

God wanted His creation to remain in His image and in His likeness. However, as a result of their disobedience, their human nature was corrupted. They were no longer wise in their decision making or perfect in their thought process, or in their actions. Their desires had turned inward and they, for the first time, experienced self-satisfaction and realized too late that their actions were displeasing to their Creator.

God was protecting them by charging them not to eat of the fateful tree, but it also would prove their faithfulness or unfaithfulness to God. It looked good, so surely it would taste good and therefore, it was desired to possibly even make one wise. They gave in to the temptation that Satan presented to them; the very house that surrounded their spirit and soul was corrupted. Their nature was corrupted and their house was no longer perfect; it was now contaminated with a sin nature. Thus, the human nature of mankind would remain sinful; a nature that could only be rectified by a divine touch from its Creator. Second man Adam, in the likeness of man but yet fully God came, in the express image of the former state of the first man Adam, to rectify man's sinful state. This will be discussed in more detail later. Not only would mankind feel the effects of the sinful state that man would endure but also all of God's creation was corrupted.

Was God displeased with His family? I am sure He was, but He did not give up on them. He was not taken by surprise. It cost the blood of an animal or two, to clothe Adam and Eve; but it did not rid them of their now sinful nature. God knew from the foundation of the world that man would fall. God only wanted people who love and serve Him from the desire of their heart, not because they were told to. He created mankind with an ability to choose to love and serve Him. He created man with a god-size vacuum in their being to hunger after Him. That vacuum has to be filled with the Spirit of God to enjoy fellowship with Him.

Before the fall, God came into the garden and walked and talked with Adam and Eve. They did not need a place to enter to worship God or talk with Him. The entire garden was holy; it was a place that God could meet with them prior to their disobedience. The garden of Eden was a place of communion, of worship. God is a personal God who met with them face to face. They were created in His image and in His likeness.

God is wise in His ways, holy in His being, and righteous in His actions and man was also created this way—to be wise in his mind, perfect in his living, and right in his actions; but sin destroyed man's ability to be, and to act as such. As a result, Adam and Eve were banned from the garden and the tree of life was protected from them so that God's family would not be eternally lost. If they would have eaten of the tree of life after their disobedience, there would be no redemption for mankind. But God, in His infinite wisdom and foreknowledge, made a way of escape through a promise He made with them. "I will put animosity between you (the serpent) and the woman, and between your descendant (the serpent's descendant) and her descendant; he will bruise your head, and you will bruise his heel" (Genesis 3:15, CJB). God knew who He was talking to, His enemy the devil. The serpent was just the devil's instrument. Nonetheless, God was not finished with His family and He was not going to let Satan destroy what He started. He had already counted the cost and knew what would have to take place to redeem His children from their sinful condition.

God started building again when Seth's son, Enos, was born. Eve was sure that it would be Abel's seed that would prepare the breech that was caused by her deception. But Cain killed Abel. Eve said at Seth's birth, "For God has granted me another seed in place of Hevel (Abel), since Kayin (Cain) killed him." It was not until Enos, Seth's son, was born that men's hearts began to cry out to God. "To Shet (Seth, meaning granted) too was born a son, whom he called Enosh (Enos). That is when people began to call on the name of ADONAI" (Genesis 4:26, CJB).

Nonetheless, the promised seed had not come, only a carrier to the next generation. Unfortunately down through the ages, men's hearts turned evil because the sinful human nature had not been taken care of. The Bible says, "In time, when men began to multiply on earth, and daughters were born to them, the sons of God saw that the daughters of men were attractive; and they took wives for themselves, whomever they chose" (Genesis 6:1–2, CJB). It was through Seth, Enos, Cainan, Mahalaleel, Jared, and Enoch from the seed of Adam who are ancestors of the promised seed down through the ages to Noah.

The remainder of the children of Seth, and his descendants, we can only assume, were also sons of God but they became involved with the daughters of men (probably the descendants of Cain) which was a "breaking down of the separation between the godly line of Seth and the godless line of Cain." There are not any other names mentioned in Seth's lineage with the exception the Scripture saying "the sons of God" which intermingled with the daughters of men. However, Christ did not quit building His household, His family.

Christ said, "I also tell you this: you are Kefa (Peter), [which means 'Rock,'] and on this rock (Christ)* I will build my Community, and the gates of Sh'ol (hell) will not overcome it" (Matthew 16:18 CJB). [1] And He is still the Rock today. Christ's household (community, family) was never destroyed and it was an emphatic statement "I will

---

1   I added Christ beside rock because 1 Corinthians 10:4, CJB, says "And they all drank from the Spirit – for they drank from a Spirit-sent Rock which followed them, and that Rock was the Messiah."

build." That actually does not mean that was the beginning but I would like to think that He was saying, "my family was not destroyed, and I will finish what I started. My family needs a house to dwell in." An example of "I will" is: I am on my way to the store, but I have a flat tire. But the flat tire will not prevent me from going to the store. I will have the tire repaired and go on to the store. Therefore I *will* go to the store; nothing is going to prevent me from going, not even a flat tire. I was just delayed for a short time, and then I continued on my way. Thus, "I will build my Community."

I will be using community, household, and house throughout. The Lord gave to me the word "house" to use in my title. I also want to explain to you why I am not using the word church. In the Hebrew language, the use is either, community, the Messiah's community or congregation. Nonetheless, we are going to look at the original meaning of church? In Greek, church is *ecclesia*, meaning "assembly, congregation, or council." In the Greek language, ecclesia was referred to as a *civil* assembly, or congregation or council. In other words, a secular meeting not a Theocratic meeting.

> In the earlier Greek writings, the Christian community was pronounced "ku-ri-a-kos" or "ku-ri-a-kon." Neither the Greek word "ecclesia" or 'kuriakon' was the correct meaning in referring to the house that Christ built or a meeting place for Believers or church. The meaning of "Ku-ri-a-kos" is understood by its root: "Ku- ri-os," which means

"lord or Lord." Thus, "kuriakos" (i.e., "church") is "pertaining to a lord or the Lord." It refers to something that pertains to, or belongs to, a lord or the Lord. However, the only time Kurios was used as the Lord in the New Testament was pertaining to the Lord's Day found in I Corinthians 11:20 where it refers to "the Lord's supper and once again in Revelation 1:10 where it refers to "the Lord's day." The Greek "kuriakos" eventually came to be used in Old English form as "cirice" (Kee-ree-ke), then "churche" (kerke), and eventually "church" in its traditional pronunciation. A church, then, is correctly something that "pertains to, or belongs to, a lord"[1] and in a civic manner and the Lord only in the two Scriptures mentioned above.

This particular definition was pertaining to a civil lord, or ruler. That is why the early Christians were persecuted because their calling out or assembly were not civil meetings; they were theocratic gatherings because Jesus was their Lord and they proclaimed it very loudly to the extent many lost their lives. "The seventy-two translators that translated the Septuagint around 280 B.C. were very much aware of that word ekklesia. They used it in the Septuagint as a replacement of the Hebrew for the "congregation of Israel."[2] The Bible I am taking Scriptures from is the Complete Jewish Bible and was written by a

Christian Jew by the name of David H. Stern. He also uses the word "congregation" or "community" instead of church.

It is true, many today refer to the Church as the body of Christ but yet it is treated like a building and not for a family (God's family) to assemble in the presence of God. Many refer to the Church as the body of Christ where believers come together to worship and see themselves as family but not all those who have accepted Christ as Lord and Savior as part of God's family.

Actually, the buildings of today that we worship in are man-made and doomed to destruction when Christ sets up His new kingdom. But the house that Christ built for the community of believers will never be destroyed. There is a perpetual covenant between God and Abraham and His seed—pertaining to God's children—which will be discussed later. However, this is my reasoning behind using community or the Messianic community versus church. Church has been so misused over the years.

I was walking throughout my house when suddenly the thought came to me: "The House that Christ Built." I pondered on that and knew that the thought came from the Lord. For this reason, I am using house instead of church. Now what do I mean by house, or I should say what does the Lord mean by house. God referred to Noah and his sons and their wives as Noah's household. "*ADONAI* said to Noach (Noah), 'Come into the ark, you and all your household; for I have seen that you alone in this generation are righteous before me'" (Genesis 7:1, CJB). God does realize what a household is and the ark was their house for several months. God's household needs a house to dwell in. Let us continue with the house that Christ built.

God's children are also referred to a building where God will house Himself. "I will house myself in them… and I will walk among you, I will be their God, and they will be my people. Therefore *ADONAI* says, 'Go out from their midst; separate yourselves; don't even touch what is unclean, Then I myself will receive you. In fact, I will be your Father, and you will be my sons and daughters, says *ADONAI-Tzva'ot* (Lord Almighty)" (2 Corinthians 6:16–18, CJB). Sons and daughters make up a household. Christ called us mother, sisters, and brothers. "Whoever does what my Father in heaven wants, that person is my brother and sister and mother" (Matthew 12:50, CJB). It definitely sounds like family to me. Let's continue.

As I was saying earlier, the house that Christ built never ceased for a moment. Yes, men's hearts were so evil; but there was one man who found grace in the eyes of the Lord. That one man was Noah, the son of Lamech, who was the son of Methuselah, who was a descendant of Enoch, who was translated to heaven because he walked with God, who was a descendant of Seth.

Just as the garden of Eden was created by God for Adam and Eve and their family to live in, there was going to be a place for Noah and his family to live in for a year. This would entail the building of an ark for the next one hundred years; however, the instructions on how to build the ark were given to Noah by God. The individuals on that ark consisted only of eight people, Noah and his household—his wife and their three sons and their wives. Not only Noah but also Shem was part of the foundation of the house that Christ was building, just as Enoch and Adam was and all the in-between lineage of Christ. Just because Adam sinned, the family that Christ created and told to procreate was not discarded. It was steadily growing. God was going to have an earthly family and nothing was going to stop it from growing. The foundation was going to be restored with the prophets, and later the apostles with Jesus Christ as the Chief Cornerstone.

What I am saying to you is such a mystery that I had to stop, and pray, and ponder before I could continue writing, but I believe you will see how it all comes together and fits perfectly in the plan of God. It truly is a mystery, but not hidden where His children cannot understand what beautiful thing we are a part of.

God wanted people who would worship Him in spirit and in truth, not just Adam and Eve, Seth, Enos, and Enos's seed and his descendants. God wanted a community of people. Remember, "the gates of hell" will not overcome His community or His household. Thus far, Christ's community of believers came from how many households. Let's see, there are Adam and Eve, Seth and Enoch and Enoch's descendants, and now Noah and Shem and Shem's descendants through Enos. Are you getting the picture? Only those who are following after the heart of God! We can see the household of God growing. It is the family of God growing up into the spiritual house that Christ built. Let's go on.

But first notice, many had fallen away from God. What happened to the sons of God who began calling on the name of the Lord when Enos was born? From Scripture, we know that men's hearts had become evil with the exception of a few, but still yet Christ's building project was underway. He will finish what He started, just as He will finish what He has started in each of His children. The only thing we know about the remainder of Seth's descendants, besides Enos, is found in the latter part of Numbers 24:17, CJB: "A scepter will arise from Isra'el, to crush the corners of Mo'av (Moab) and destroy all descendants of Shet (Seth)." The Moabites were descendants of Lot and his firstborn daughter; and the remainder of Seth's descendants, sons of God intermingled with the daughters of men, the Cainites. This is for study at another time. As mentioned, I am basically covering the lineage of Christ from Adam to the birth of Christ, and I am not mentioning all the lineage of Christ, just those who most everyone is familiar with.[2]

The next major event took place when once again men's hearts were full of evil and idol worship was very prominent. But on each occasion, God chooses someone who will follow His directions, and His family continues to grow.

---

2   I am not saying all those not mentioned were not part of God's house, but they were not the foundation. I am giving the lineage of the seed of Christ, the foundation of His house, and the offspring of His family that was started with Adam and Eve. We do know that it was only by faith that anyone was made a part of God's family from Adam to Christ Jesus—only those who believed in the coming Messiah which was prophesied from the very beginning in the garden of Eden and carried down through the ages; first orally, then written by Moses. I am not going to say that the remainder of these men's seed did not live by faith, only God knows. There are names scattered throughout the Old Testament of men and women who lived by faith or was blessed by God—Ishmael, Jabez, Esther, Mordecai, Job, just to name a few.

Now ADONAI said to Avram (Abram), "Get yourself
out of your country, away from your kinsmen and
away from your father's house, and go to the land that
I will show you. I will make of you a great nation, I
will bless you, and I will make your name great; and
you are to be a blessing. I will bless those who bless you,
but I will curse anyone who curses you; and by you all
the families of the earth will be blessed.

—Genesis 12:1–3, CJB

3

The Building Covenant

The house that Christ built was about to take off in an entirely different direction which would include building a nation—a new nation known as the Hebrew nation. God visited people who were steeped in idolatry. People who had fallen so far from God that they worshiped practically everything but God. It was nothing for them to sacrifice their children to their gods. Nonetheless, God chose a man from Haran to continue His building project. God visited and told Abram, a descendant eighteen generations from Seth, to leave his country, his kinsmen, and his father's house, and go where He would lead him. If Abram would go, God told him that he would make of him a great nation. God further told him that He would bless those who bless him.

So by faith, Abram left his country; his kinsmen, with the exception of Lot and Lot's wife; and his father's house and started traveling toward Canaan. Abram, who was later called Abram the Hebrew (meaning a nation, see Genesis 14:13, CJB), obeyed God; but probably couldn't comprehend the idea that God would make of him a great nation since he did not have any children. He and his wife, Sarai, were of great age; actually, he was ninety; and Sarai was well beyond childbearing years.

But with God, nothing is impossible. God made a covenant with Abram that the land of Canaan would be given to his seed. (See Genesis 12:7, CJB) God confirmed His everlasting covenant with Abram by having Abram bring to Him specifically detailed types of animals (See Genesis 15:9, CJB). "He brought him all these, cut the animals in two and placed the pieces opposite each other; but he didn't cut the birds in half, Birds of prey swooped down on the carcasses, but Avram (Abram) drove them away" (Genesis 15:10, 11, CJB). When the sun set, Abram fell into a deep sleep and a thick darkness surrounded him. Verse 17b, 18, reveals the covenant being made between God and Abram and his descendants. "A smoking fire pot and a flaming torch (God) appeared, which passed between these animal parts. That day *ADONAI* made a covenant with Avram: 'I have given this land to your descendants'" (Genesis15:10–18, CJB). God proceeded to tell Abram the extent of the land that would be his and his descendants (See Genesis 15:18b–21).

The Hebrew nation (Christ's household) was about to be set apart from all others.[1] Reason being, God found a man in Haran, who was willing to leave everything and walk by faith to a land of promise. God had called Abram's father Terah to go—"Terach (Terah) took his son Avram, his son Haran's son Lot, and Sarai his daughter-in-law, his son Avram's wife; and they left Ur of the Kasdim (Chaldees) to go to the land of Kena'an (Canaan). But when they came to Haran, they stayed there" (Genesis 11:31, CJB). We don't know why Terah stopped in Haran, but we do know that it was in the plan of God that someone would go to Canaan and Abram, Terah's son, ended up being that man.

With the knowledge of knowing that Abram was to bear a child, and Sarah not believing it would be her because of her age, she decided to help God out. Sarah gave to

---

1   The descendants of Joseph, Jesus's earthly father can be traced back to Judah, the son of Jacob, the son of Isaac, the son of Abraham. Mary's descendants, the mother of Jesus, can be traced back to the first man Adam, the son of God, our Creator, who breathed the breath of life into Adam. Jesus's birth was of a preternatural influence when the power of the Highest overshadowed her and planted the divine seed in her womb. "The *Ruach HaKodesh* (Holy Ghost will come over you, the power of *Ha 'Elyon* (the Most High) will cover you. Therefore the holy child born to you will be called the Son of God" (Luke 1:35, CJB). Therefore, the second Man Adam was born.

Abram, her servant, Hagar, to birth Abram a son. In their culture, when a woman was barren it was customary for the husband to birth a child through the servant or slave that belonged to his wife. Hagar did produce Abram a son— Ishmael (meaning "whom God hears").

Nonetheless, nine years later, God Almighty appeared to Abram and once again confirmed the covenant between Himself and Abram as an everlasting covenant and by the same time the following year, Sarai would bear a son whose name would be called Yitz'chak (Isaac) "laughter." During this time, God changed Abram (exalted father) to Abraham—"father of many" and Sarai (mockery) was changed to Sarah "princess"… she would become a mother of nations (See Genesis 17:5, 15, 19, cjb). The covenant was confirmed by circumcision. Not only did Abraham circumcise the foreskin of his own flesh at the age of ninety-nine, but all who dwelt in his household and anyone bought with money, which was not of his seed. This is very important which will be explained later.

God promised Abraham that the covenant would be established also with Isaac and his seed. The child had to be birthed by Sarah, Abraham's wife. Nonetheless, God blessed Ishmael. He too was circumcised at the age of thirteen; therefore, he also was blessed by God but not with the same blessing as Isaac. His blessing was he would begat twelve princes, and God would make him a great nation.

Even though Ishmael and his mother Hagar had to leave Abraham's household, after Isaac was weaned, God would not forget him. He heard his cry in the wilderness, when he and his mother had to leave the household of Abraham. "God heard the boy's voice, and the angel of God called to Hagar from heaven and said to her. 'What's wrong with you, Hagar? Don't be afraid, because God has heard the voice of the boy in his present situation. Get up, lift the boy up, and hold him tightly in your hand, because I am going to make him a great nation'" (Genesis 21:17, 18, CJB).

"God was with the boy, and he grew" (verse 20a). He lived in the desert and became an archer. He lived in the Pa'ran Desert, and his mother chose a wife for him from the land of Egypt. Aah, the land of Egypt, the country that Joseph was taken to and used to save the Hebrew children from starvation and also where Moses was born to lead his people out of bondage. The plan of God is beyond our comprehension. Let's move on. But not before I mention that Isaac and Ishmael buried Abraham. Ties were not completely severed between Abraham and Ishmael and his brother Isaac.[2]

---

2   Ishmael died at the age of 137 in the presence of all his people, but not before his wife birthed Ishmael twelve tribal rulers as God had promised. How good is God? Actually the same number of tribes that God blessed Jacob with. Ishmael's descendants also are mentioned in Scripture.

To comfort Isaac during his time of mourning over the death of his mother, Abraham sent his servant to his kindred in Paddan-Aram and told him to bring a wife back for his son. The family of Rebekah gave a profound blessing over her before she left with Abraham's servant. "Our sister, may you be the mother of millions, and may your descendants possess the cities of those who hate them" (Genesis 24:60, CJB). The servant brought Rebekah, the daughter of B'tu'el (Bethuel) son of Nachor, Abraham's brother, to Isaac. At the age of forty, Isaac took Rebekah as his wife into his mother's tent, and he loved her. He was comforted from the loss of his mother.

When Isaac was sixty years old, Rebekah conceived and carried twins in her womb. There was a battle within her womb between the babies, so much so that she inquired of the Lord, who answered her. "There are two nations in your womb. From birth they will be two rival peoples. One of these peoples will be stronger than the other, and the older will serve the younger" (Genesis 25:23, CJB). Esau, meaning "hairy", was the firstborn with Jacob holding to Esau's heel (meaning "he supplants") when he was delivered.

Eventually, Esau sold his birthright as the firstborn to Jacob when he came in from the "open country exhausted" begging Jacob for a bowl of his "red stuff." "Then Ya'akov (Jacob) gave him bread and lentil stew; he ate and drank, got up and went on his way. Thus 'Esav (Esau) showed how little he valued his birthright" (Genesis 25:34, CJB). Jacob supplants or supersedes Esau's rights as the firstborn. And of course it was Jacob who received Esau, the firstborn's blessing, when he tricked their father into eating his meal by dressing as Esau and smelling like Esau. The blessing was, "See, my son smells like a field which *ADONAI* has blessed. So may God give you dew from heaven, the richness of the earth, and grain and wine in abundance. May peoples serve you and nations bow down to you. May you be lord over your kinsmen, let your mother's descendants bow down to you. Cursed be everyone who curses you, and blessed be everyone who blesses you" (Genesis 27:27b–29, cjb)!

> The 'birthright' had three elements: (1) Until the establishment of the Aaronic priesthood the head of the family exercised priestly rights. (2) The Abrahamic family held the Edemic promise of the Satan-Bruiser (Gen. 3:15)—Abel, Seth, Shem, Abraham, Isaac, Esau. (3) Esau, as the firstborn, was in the direct line of the Abrahamic promise of the Earth-Blesser (Gen. 12:3). For all that was revealed, in Esau might have been fulfilled those two great Messianic promises. This birth-right Esau sold for a momentary fleshly gratification. Jacob's conception of the birthright at that time was, doubtless, carnal and inadequate, but his desire for it evidenced true faith.[3]

Thus the turmoil begins. Jacob left Be'er-Sheva and went toward Haran because of Esau's hatred toward him. On the way to Haran, he spent the night in a certain place and dreamed of a ladder and an angel of the Lord ascending and descending on it.[3]

> Then suddenly *ADONAI* (Lord) was standing there next to him; and he said, "I am *ADONAI*, the God of Avraham your [grand] father and the God of Yitz'chak (Isaac). The land on which you are lying I will give to you and to your descendants. Your descendants will be as numerous as the grains of dust on the earth. You will expand to the west and to the east, to the north and to the south. By you and your descendants all the families of the earth will be blessed. Look, I am with you. I will guard you wherever you go, and I will bring you back into this land, because I won't leave you until I have done what I have promised you." Jacob awoke from his sleep and said, "Truly, *ADONAI* is in this place – and I didn't know it!" Then he became afraid and said, "This place is fearsome! This has to be the house of God! This is the gate of heaven.
>
> Genesis 28:13–17 (CJB)

---

3 Jesus spoke to Nathanael basically the same thing that Jacob saw, and Jacob called the place Bethel, meaning house of God. Jesus said Nathanael would see "The angels of God going up and coming down on the son of Man!" (See John 1:51). Jesus is our Bethel. This will become more clearly as you read. Jesus truly is the gate of heaven. However, with Jacob, the Lord stood at the top of the ladder. The Son of Man would descend to earth to continue building His house. And that He did.

God had chosen Jacob while in His mother's womb and He was going to increase the house of God through his descendants and one (Jesus Christ) of his descendants would be the gateway into heaven. Everyone under the covenant of Abraham's household—including Ishmael and Abraham's servants, Isaac and now Jacob and his descendants—would receive this blessing *if* they lived by faith. Paul said in Romans 9:6–8, CJB: "But the present condition of Isra'el does not mean that the Word of God has failed. For not everyone from Isra'el is truly part of Isra'el; indeed, not all the descendants are seed of Avraham; rather What is to be called your 'seed' will be in Yitz'chak (Isaac)." Many children were born from the seed of Abraham, and not all of his children were from the seed that would produce the heir that would save and unite God's people. The seed from Isaac would be Jacob that would be in the lineage of Jesus Christ. Thus God visited Jacob and renewed His covenant with him. (Also see verses 8–13)

Jacob continued on to Haran and worked for Laban fourteen years to have his two wives. Jacob agreed to work for Laban, his mother's brother, seven years to receive Rachel, Laban's daughter, as his wife. But instead, he was tricked into taking Leah, the eldest daughter of Laban, for his wife. Because of her veil, he was not aware of who she was until the following morning. He agreed to work seven more years to have the woman he truly loved, Rachel. Thus, a week later, he also took Rachel to be his wife.

God saw that Leah was "unloved so He made her fertile, while Rachel remained childless." Leah was delighted for her first son, believing that Jacob would then love her. She named him Ruben (meaning "see, a son!"). She again was with child and named him Simeon (meaning "hearing") because God knew that she was unloved. She again was with child and named him Levi (meaning "joining") just knowing that she would win her husband's heart. She once again was with child and named him Judah (meaning "praise") because, regardless of the outcome whether loved or not, from her month was praises for God. She did not bare anymore children until much later.

Jesus Christ would be born from the lineage of Judah. Ironically from the one whose name means "praise." "Y'hudah (Judah) is a lion's cub; my son, you stand over the prey. He crouches down and stretches like a lion; like a lioness, who dares to provoke him? The scepter will not pass from Y'hudah, nor the ruler's staff from between his legs, until he comes to whom [obedience] belongs (or: until Shiloh comes KJV) and it is he whom the peoples will obey" (Genesis 49:9, 10, CJB).

Rachel gave to Jacob her handmaiden Bilhah and she conceived twice; and Rachel named them Dan (he judged) and Naftali (Naphtali, my wrestling). Leah gave her handmaiden Zilpah to Jacob as his wife, and she conceived twice. Leah named them Gad (good fortune) and Asher (happy). God opened Leah's womb again and she conceived twice more. Leah named them Yissakhar (Issachar, heir, reward) and Z'vulun (Zebulun, living together). Then God opened Rachel's womb, and she conceived and named him Yosef (Joseph, may he add) and much later conceived again and Jacob named him Benjamin (son of the right hand, son of the south).

After twenty years with Laban, Jacob, his wives, and his wives' two slave girls, his servants, and his eleven children with all their belongings left and was on their way when Jacob sent his messengers ahead of him to Esau. His messengers returned and told him that Esau was coming to meet him. Jacob became afraid, divided his family and his animals, and sent them in different directions and he cried out to the God of his father. He spent the night alone. The following morning, he sent his messengers off with a very sizeable gift to give to his brother. He then gathered his family and sent them across the ford Jabbok. He stayed behind and spent the night wrestling with a man. The man could not defeat Jacob and Jacob would not let him go until the man blessed him. The man said, "From now on, you will no longer be called Ya'akov (Jacob), but Isra'el: because you have shown your strength to both God and men and have prevailed" Genesis 32:29 (28), CJB. Jacob called the place Peniel (face of God) because he had seen God face to face, and yet lived.

After his successful encounter with his brother Esau, he traveled to Succoth and built a house there. Jacob then went to Shalem, in the land of Canaan and purchased a parcel of land from Hamor in Kena'an; he set up camp and built an altar, which he called El-Elohei-Yisra'el (God, the God of Isra'el).

If you look back over Jacob's family, they were not innocent people. They had idols among them; his sons committed whoredom; and Dinah, Jacob and Leah's daughter, was defiled by the Hitite, Sh'khem (Shechem), the son of Hamor. And as a result, Shim'on and Levi, Dinah's brothers, slaughtered all the menfolk of that city. Afterward, "Ya'akov (Jacob) said to Shim'on (Simon) and Levi, 'You have caused me trouble by making me stink in the opinion of the local inhabitants, the Kena'ani (Caananites) and the P'rizi (Perizzites). Since I don't have many people, they'll align themselves together against me and attack me; and I will be destroyed, I and my household.' They replied, 'Should we let our sister be treated like a whore'" (Genesis 34:30, 31, CJB). Afterward, God spoke to Jacob and told him to return to Bethel.

> God said to Ya'akov, Get up, go up to Beit-El (Bethel) and live there, and make there an altar to God, who appeared to you when you fled 'Esav your brother." Then Ya'akov said to his household and all the others with him, "Get rid of the foreign gods

that you have with you, purify yourselves, and put on fresh clothes. We're going to move on and go up to Beit-El. There I will build an altar to God, who answered me when I was in such distress and stayed with me wherever I went."

Genesis 35:1–3 (cjb)

Jacob got rid of all the idols that were among his people and returned to the place that he called the house of God, the gate to heaven. Generations later, Isaiah reminded the children of Israel what God had done through their forefather Jacob. Isaiah 29:22, 23, cjb proclaims, "Therefore, here are the words of *ADONAI*, who redeemed Avraham, concerning the house of Ya'akov: 'Ya'akov will no longer be ashamed, no longer will his face grow pale. When his descendants see the work of my hands among them, they will consecrate my name. Yes, they will consecrate the Holy one of Ya'akov and stand in awe of the God of Isra'el.'"

God's house will truly enlarge itself. God is true to His covenant. God appeared to Jacob and blessed him and said to him, "Your name is Ya'akov, but you will be called Ya'akov no longer; your name will be Isra'el." God further said to him, "I am El Shaddai. Be fruitful and multiply. A nation, indeed a group of nations, will come from you; kings will be descended from you. Moreover, the land which I gave to Avraham and Yitzchak I will give to you, and I will give the land to your descendants after you" (Genesis 35:10–12,

CJB). Thus, the perpetual covenant is once again recorded with Abraham's seed just as it was with Isaac, but this time with Jacob, the seed bearer of Christ, through his son Judah.

Why is all this information significant, you might ask? The significance is that it is important to know that God made this covenant with Abraham and His seed, and circumcision was established as a sign of that covenant. What does this have to do with today? Everything that took place before the law and under the law was fulfilled by Jesus Christ including circumcision. This will be covered in more detail in a later chapter. Before the law, tithing was established and circumcision was a commitment; and after Christ the law was fulfilled, tithe was to be brought to the storehouse, and circumcision is of the heart through the shed blood of Jesus. Nonetheless, Jesus, a Jew, was circumcised according to the covenant between God and Abraham. We too have to be circumcised, but it is a cutting off of sin from our very being, the heart of man: the center of his being. This enables us to become a part of the household of God and family members into the house that Christ built.

God walked and talked with Adam and Eve in the garden but because of their disobedience, they were no longer permitted in His house. Nonetheless, they were expected to build an altar and offer sacrifices. Apparently repentance was done on their part because Abel is an example of that form of worship. The first thing that Noah did when they departed from the ark was build an altar to the Lord and offer burnt offerings on the altar. (See Genesis 8:20, CJB) In the wilderness, God established a place, such as the tent of meeting, for His glory to fill, and to meet with His children, and sacrifices to be made. It was not until Solomon that a temple was built for God's presence to dwell and a meeting place for His children, but still yet sacrifices were to be made. Jesus Christ died as a sacrifice outside the gate of Jerusalem for our atonement and sanctification, just as animals were slaughtered outside the gate to cover the sins of the nation of Israel.

Adam and Eve communed with God in the garden of Eden. In the wilderness, the tent of meeting was set up when they were not traveling to commune with God. In Jesus's day, synagogues and temples were the meeting places. Today we meet in churches. Through Christ, every day is a day of worship to God because Christ is our Sabbath. "Then he said to them, '*Shabbat* (Sabbath) was made for mankind, not mankind for *Shabbat*; So the Son of Man is Lord even of *Shabbat*'" (Mark 2:27, 28, CJB).

God loves people and He wants people to love Him in return today as He did during the Old Testament and New Testament times. I do not want to get ahead of myself. Therefore, I am returning to the building aspect of God's house with the understanding it all started at the very beginning of time and will be completed at the end of the Gentile world system when He returns for his household of believers—His mothers and His brothers and sisters.

We will pick up where Jacob's son, Joseph, was sold into slavery to the Midianites merchantmen and taken to Egypt. As a result, Potiphar, an officer of pharaoh's court purchased Joseph from the Ishmaelites who had brought him there. We understand the reason he was sold into slavery by Joseph himself as he was talking to his brethren after their father Jacob's death. "You meant to do me harm, but God meant it for good—so that it would come about as it is today, with many people's lives being saved" (Genesis 50:20, CJB). Satan meant to destroy God's sovereign plan of redemption but God meant it for good—"with many people's lives being saved."

It is important to note prior to Jacob's death, he blessed his sons. Each one received a blessing, but the one that I will mention is the blessing that Judah received. "The scepter will not pass from Y'hudah, (Judah) nor the ruler's staff from between his legs, until he comes to whom [obedience] belongs[4] and it is he whom the peoples will obey" (Genesis 49:10, CJB). This scripture is prophecy of Jesus Christ. The

---

4   Or until Shiloh comes.

lineage of Christ is from the seed of Judah and Tamar's son, Pharez; the ancestor of both Mary and Joseph. (See Matthew 1:2, 3 and Luke 3:33, 34) At this time, God's household was a total of threescore and ten in Egypt. (See Genesis 46:26, 27). His house was still being built. The foundation was surely getting larger and His family was growing.

After the death of God's three patriarchs—Abraham, Isaac and Jacob (Israel)—their seed remained in Egypt. By the time that new kings who did not know anything about Joseph had ruled, and the Hebrew children were to leave Egypt, the Scripture says, "Yosef died, as did all his brothers and all that generation. The descendants of Isra'el were fruitful, increased abundantly, multiplied and grew very powerful; the land became filled with them" (Exodus 1:6, 7, cjb). As you can see, the household of God has increased abundantly but His household was in terrible trouble.

Now there arose a new king over Egypt. He knew nothing about Yosef but said to his people, "Look, the descendants of Isra'el have become a people too numerous and powerful for us. Come, let's use wisdom in dealing with them. Otherwise, they'll continue to multiply; and in the event of war they might ally themselves with our enemies, fight against us and leave the land altogether."

—Exodus 1:8–10, cjb

4

The Plight of God's Children

The Hebrew children were in Egypt for four hundred years. Several kings/pharaohs sat on the throne in Egypt that did not know Joseph. When the Hebrew children arrived in Egypt there were only seventy of the household of God. Can we even fathom how many there were at the time that the Hebrew children started experiencing slavery some four hundred years later? Many scholars believe there were possibly around six million Jews at the time of their exodus out of Egypt. That I suppose is an assumption. No matter, they were as the stars in the sky standing out as no other people.

> So they put slavemasters over them to oppress them with forced labor, and they built for Pharaoh the storage cities of Pitom (Pithom) and Ra'amses. But the more the Egyptians oppressed them, the more they multiplied and expanded, until the Egyptians

came to dread the people of Isra'el and worked them relentlessly, making their lives bitter with hard labor—digging clay, making bricks, all kinds of field work; and in all this toil they were shown no mercy.

Exodus 1:11–14 (CJB)

Not only were they shown no mercy regarding labor, the midwives for the Hebrew women were told to kill all Hebrew boys. But because they were God-fearing women, they refused. The midwives reason, when asked, was the Hebrew women were different and they delivered quickly before they arrived to help. Because of their stance against the pharaoh, the midwives prospered and so did the Hebrew children.

Nonetheless, the pharaoh ordered his people to throw all the newborn Hebrew boys in the river, but the girls were allowed to live. As a result, a couple who were descendants from the family of Levi hid their youngest son in a waterproof basket and set him afloat with his sister watching. The pharaoh's daughter saw the basket in the reeds and told her maids to bring it to her. When the princess saw the baby crying she had pity on him. The baby's sister came forward and asked if she would like a Hebrew woman to nurse the baby, and the pharaoh's daughter told her "yes." So the sister went for her mother. The pharaoh's daughter told the mother, "Take this child away, and nurse it for me, and I will pay you for doing it. So the woman took the child and nursed it" (Exodus 2:9, CJB).

When the child had "grown some", the mother took him to the pharaoh's daughter and she raised him as her son. "She called him Moshe [pull out]," (Moses) explaining, "Because I pulled him out of the water." After he became an adult, he visited his kinsmen and saw how they were being mistreated by the Egyptians. As a result, he slew an Egyptian who was abusing one of the Hebrew children. The following day, he once again visited his kinsmen and saw them fighting among themselves and he asked why were they against one another. One responded by asking him, "Who appointed you ruler and judge over us? Do you intend to kill me the way you killed the Egyptian?" (Exodus 2:14, cjb)

Moses became afraid and fled into the land of Midian because he feared what the pharaoh might do to him. While in exile for forty years, Moses married and had sons, one whose name was Gershom (meaning "expulsion"). In the meantime back in Egypt, the pharaoh died but the people were still being abused. God heard their cry and remembered His covenant with Abraham, Isaac, and Jacob. While Moses was tending his father-in-law's sheep on the far side of the desert, he went up into the mountain of Horeb. An angel of the Lord appeared to Moses in the midst of a burning bush. He went to approach the bush and he heard a voice that said, "Moshe! Moshe…, don't come any closer! Take your sandals off your feet, because the place where you are standing is holy ground. I am the God of your father…the God of Avraham, the God of Yitz'chak and the God of Ya'akov…" He continued with, "I have seen how my people are being oppressed in Egypt and heard their cry for release from their slavemasters, because I know their pain. I have come down to rescue them from the Egyptians and to bring them up out of that country to a good and spacious land, a land flowing with milk and honey…" (Exodus 3:4–8, CJB). God chose Moses to lead His children out of Egypt.

God calls them "my people" and He chose Moses to lead them. Was Moses ready to go? No, he was not. He gave his excuses even so far as to say he was not a good speaker but God would not accept his excuses. Actually, God became angry with Moses after He explained to him what to do to convince His people that God sent him. Nonetheless, God told him that his brother Aaron was a good speaker, and he was on his way to meet him. Aaron would be his mouthpiece and say what God instructed Moses to tell him to relate to the Hebrew children. God was not only preparing Moses, He was also preparing Aaron as the spiritual leader for His family while they were traveling throughout their wonderings.

God also told Moses that He would harden the pharaoh's heart and the pharaoh would refuse to let them go; and when he refuses, Moses was to tell him, "*ADONAI* says,

'Isra'el is my firstborn son. I have told you to let my son go in order to worship me, but you have refused to let him go. Well, then, I will kill your firstborn son'" (Exodus 4:22, 23, CJB)! God is speaking to Moses that Israel is His firstborn son—God's family, God's household which makes up the house that Christ built. God is Israel's Father.[1]

God told Moses to tell His people when Moses feared that his people would not listen to him, "*Ehyeh Ashere Ehyeh* [I am/will be what I am/will be] (KJV—I AM THAT I AM)" and added, "here is what to say to the people of Isra'el: *'Ehyeh* [I Am or I Will Be] (KJV—I AM) has sent me to you.'" He further told Moses to tell them:

> *ADONAI*, the God of your fathers, the God of Avraham, Yitz'chak and Ya'akov, has sent me to you.' This is my name forever; this is how I am to be remembered generation after generation. Go, gather the leaders of Isra'el together, and say to them, '*ADONAI*, the God of your fathers, the God of Avraham, Yitz'chak and Ya'akov, has appeared to me and said, "I have been paying close attention

---

1 Jesus Christ is of the seed of Israel, God's firstborn son under covenant. God's son, Adam, is also considered His firstborn son and referred to in Scripture as first man Adam. But because of the sin of Adam, Jesus Christ, second Man Adam, lineage from His firstborn son Israel will pay the penalty of sin for His children.

to you and have seen what is being done to you in Egypt; and I have said that I will lead you up out of the misery of Egypt to the land of Kena'ani, Hitti, Emori, P'rizi, Hivi and Y'vusi, (Canaanites, and the Hittites, and the Amorites, and the Perizzites, and the Hivites, and the Jebusites KJV) to a land flowing with milk and honey.

Exodus 3:14–17 (CJB)

God was keeping his covenant. However, when Moses, his wife, and their sons were on their way to Egypt, they stopped at an inn. "At a lodging-place on the way, *ADONAI* met Moshe and would have killed him, had not Tzipporah (Zipporah, Moses' wife) taken a flintstone and cut off the foreskin of her son (Moses). She threw it at his feet, saying, 'What a bloody bridegroom you are for me?' but then, God let Moshe be. She added, 'A bloody bridegroom because of the circumcision'" (Exodus 4:24–26). Somewhere between the time that Moses and his family left Jethro, he realized that he needed to be circumcised and he had his wife do it. At some point after this, Moses sent Zipporah and the boys away and they returned to Jethro because later you will see where Jethro brings Zipporah and their sons back to Moses.[2]

When Moses approached his people, they believed. Then Moses and Aaron went unto the pharaoh but he refused to let them go. He made it harder on the Hebrew children and refused to give them straw to build their bricks. They were to find it on their own, but yet the pharaoh expected them to produce the same amount of bricks as before. As a result, not only was the pharaoh angry with the people but the people were angry with Moses and Aaron.

But God was not finished with His household, and He had a place for His family to continue being built and it was not in Egypt. It was in the land of Canaan, where milk and honey flowed: a place that God established for His children to reside. It was not going to be easy but the land was covenanted to them, and God would help them establish their families in the land as He had promised to Abraham, Isaac, and Jacob. God is a covenant keeper and was faithful in helping His children through thick and

---

2   Why is Moses being circumcised significant? It is because all those in God's family were under covenant and they had to be circumcised. And Moses was about to enter among God's family as a leader! Moses had not been circumcised because he had been raised in the pharaoh's household, he grew up among an unclean people.

thin, and He was going to help them settle in what was to be their homeland for all eternity. However, it would not be easy because God was dealing with a rebellious and stiff-necked people. But that did not stop the Lord from building His household. He knew the end result would be for all eternity.

But Pharaoh replied, "Who is ADONAI, that I should obey when he says to let Isra'el go? I don't know ADONAI, and I also won't let Isra'el go."

—Exodus 5:2, CJB

5

Let My People Go

Moses and Aaron returned to God discouraged, because neither the people nor the pharaoh would listen to them. The Lord reminded Moses that He would take care of the pharaoh; he and Aaron were to obey His command and go once again before the people and repeat what God told them. As instructed, Moses and Aaron returned to the people, but they still would not listen because they too were discouraged and oppressed. The hard labor that the pharaoh forced on them after Moses's first encounter with the pharaoh made the people hard toward Moses. So God told Moses and Aaron to go back to the pharaoh and tell him to let His people go.

God encouraged Moses and Aaron. "I have put you in the place of God to Pharaoh, and Aharon your brother will be your prophet. You are to say everything I order you, and Aharon your brother is to speak to Pharaoh and tell him to let the people of Isra'el leave his land" (Exodus 7:1, 2, cjb).

They returned to the pharaoh and said and did exactly what God told them. And sure enough, the pharaoh wanted a miracle. Aaron threw down his rod and it became a serpent, and the pharaoh's magician did likewise. Moses and Aaron returned to the pharaoh again when he was by the riverbank early in the morning. God wanted the pharaoh to understand who he was dealing with, the God of the Hebrews. Aaron was to hold his hand out over all the water supply including the river and it would turn to blood. Because of the pharaoh's hardheartedness, Aaron did as the Lord commanded. The pharaoh's magicians did the same.

God used several plagues against the pharaoh to convince him to let His people go; but he refused. Nonetheless, God told Moses to rise early and go to the pharaoh and say to him:

> Here is what *ADONAI* says: "Let my people go, so that they can worship me. For this time, I will inflict my plagues on you, yourself, and on your officials and your people; so that you will realize that I am without equal in all the earth. By now I could have stretched out my hand and struck you and your people with such severe plagues that you would have been wiped off the earth. But it is for this very reason that I have kept you alive—to show you my power, and so that my name may resound throughout the whole earth."
>
> Exodus 9:13b–16 (CJB)

The pharaoh would not concede. God sent thunder and hail and fire on the earth where the Egyptians were. The pharaoh entreated Moses to plead for him because he and his people were wrong and Moses's God was right, and Moses did so and the thunder and hail ceased.

God again hardened the pharaoh's heart so that He could demonstrate to His people miracles that they would talk about for years to come and know that He truly was God. Moses and Aaron once again went before the pharaoh asking to let God's people go. This time, the pharaoh wanted to know who all would go. When Moses stated that everyone and everything would go, including their women and children, and their animals for sacrifice, the pharaoh said "no." God released a deadly plague of locusts throughout the land of Egypt. The locusts completely covered everything on the outside—trees and plants were destroyed. And again, the pharaoh called for Moses and Aaron and repented of his sin. And again Moses interceded for him. The pharaoh's heart was hardened and refused to let them go.

Moses stretched out his hand upward and the ninth plague began. Total darkness came upon all the Egyptians. For three days, there was such a thick darkness that no one could go anywhere. This plague brought the pharaoh to agree to let all the Hebrew children go worship their God with a condition. They were to leave their animals and livestock behind. This was not possible; Moses was to take everything. When the pharaoh was told that everyone including their animals would go, this angered him. The pharaoh said to them, "Get away from me! And you had better not see my face again, because the day you see my face, you will die!" Moshe answered, "Well spoken! I will see your face no more" (Exodus 10: 28, 29, cjb). Pharaoh had sealed his own and his kingdom's fate.

God was going to bring one more plague on the Egyptians—a plague that would cause tremendous pain for every household in Egypt. The plague would be the death of every firstborn; every household and every animal would be affected. Moses and Aaron would not see Pharaoh again. But with this plague, God gave Moses instructions for His children so they would be spared from the Egyptians' fate.

With the other plagues, not one Hebrew family was affected. Their water remained pure; they were not affected by any frogs, lice, flies, illness (Murrain, kjv); neither were they affected by boils, hail, and locusts; and in every house there was light whereas in the Egyptian houses not anyone could see because of the thick darkness.

In preparation to leave in regard to the last plague, God told Moses to have every Hebrew man and woman ask their Egyptian neighbor for gold and silver jewelry. God made the Egyptians favor the Hebrews and they gave their jewelry. "*ADONAI* made the Egyptians favorably disposed toward the people. Moreover, Moshe was regarded by Pharaoh's servants and the people as a very great man in the land of Egypt" (Exodus 11:3, cjb).

The tenth and final plague was about to take place. God required that the Hebrew children prepare for what would come upon Egypt so they would not be affected. Moses and Aaron gave God's instructions to His people.

You are to begin your calendar with this month; it will be the first month of the year for you.

—Exodus 12:2, cjb

6

New Beginning

It takes a strong leader to realize when he is wrong and that the pharaoh was not. He would say he had sinned and was wrong, but when it came down to it, he was not repentant. Of course, we also know that God hardened his heart in order for God's glory to be revealed to His people. And the last plague that will befall the pharaoh and his people will not change his mind. His heart will once again be hardened, but the power of God that is displayed goes beyond any miracle or power we can comprehend. But before the miracle, God's people will come to realize the importance in the power of the blood. The blood that will be shed from the purest animal will be a start of a new beginning for the Hebrew children.

I covered several of events that happened prior to the Hebrew children leaving to show that nothing would deter Christ from building His household. Absolutely nothing! Let us get back to the "New Beginning."

Their calendar would mark a new beginning for them. "You are to begin your calendar with this month; it will be the first month of the year for you" (Exodus 12:2, CJB). And on the tenth day of the first month, Aviv (Abib), the men were to take a perfect young male lamb or goat and keep it until the fourteenth day of the month. On that day at dusk, the entire congregation would come together to slaughter the animal(s). They would then take the blood and smear it on each side of their door frame and on the frame over the door at the entrance where they would eat the meal. They were to roast the entire animal with fire and eat it with unleavened bread and bitter herbs. They were to eat every morsel, and if they couldn't, they were to burn the leftover.

They were to eat the meal fully clothed, with their shoes on and their staff in their hand ready to leave in haste because the Lord was going to make a distinction between Egypt and His people. He was going to bring judgment upon the pharaoh and everyone in his kingdom. The judgment would be that the death angel would pass over Egypt and kill every firstborn, whether man or animal. And if blood was applied on the door frames of the Hebrew children, the Lord would pass over them.

Even in the deliverance of His people, God did not forget the firstborn of the Egyptians that would die. All of Israel's firstborn would represent all of Egypt's firstborn who died. God told Moses, "Set aside for me all the firstborn. Whatever is first from the womb among the people of Isra'el, both of humans and of animals, belongs to me" (Exodus 13:2, CJB).

The Hebrew children were instructed to remember the fourteenth day of the first month, Abib, as a perpetual celebration as a remembrance of the Lord's Passover. And in remembrance, they were to observe it for seven days and during those days, there was not to be found any leaven in any of their households. Leaven represented the "sense of greedily devouring for sweetness or fermented."[4] In other words, leaven represents sin. Therefore, on the seventh day, they were to celebrate their deliverance out of bondage eating only unleavened bread during those seven days and observe the Lord's Passover thereafter with unleavened bread.

Moses informed the Hebrew children that since the firstborn male of every Egyptian household would die when the death angel passed over; every Hebrew household whose house was protected by the blood on their door frames was to give their firstborn male to God, both man and animal.

God also told Moses that their slaves who were bought with money could take part in the Lord's Passover if they so desired; only if they were circumcised. Furthermore, the foreigners and strangers who wanted to partake in the Passover also would have every man and man-child of their household circumcised. Why is this significant to understand? God was increasing His household, even with strangers and foreigners (Gentiles), if they were willing to be obedient to God's laws; their agreeing to this would be a sign of faith.

In the New Testament, Paul was chosen by Christ to reach out to the Gentiles, but it did not begin in the New Testament times. According to Moses, Gentiles who were willing to follow after God who lived among the Hebrew children were welcome into their household. Adam and Eve were the ones who were to multiply seed to worship God but they failed to keep God's law—to not eat of the tree of knowledge of good and evil. Nonetheless, because of sin entering into the world, we must remember the covenant was between Abraham and his descendants and God. Everyone entering into or taking part in this covenant is by faith. We too enter into the new covenant by faith through Jesus Christ.

Christ will increase His household with all who will have a circumcision of the heart—an acknowledgement that sin is at the door of their soul because of the sinful nature from Adam and Eve's disobedience; and if Christ's blood is applied to the door post of their heart (being) through repentance, He will pass over them at judgment. Those who live among the children of light and are obedient to Christ's commands are also welcomed into the family of

God through faith. Jesus's prayer in John 17:20, 21a, cjb was, "I pray not only for these, but also for those who will trust in me because of their word, that they may all be one." Jesus was praying for His own people and for those who would trust Him through their word. And through Peter and Paul, Gentiles received their word.

God has included individuals who were not of the descendants of Abraham to become part of the household that He was building. We can see this taking shape down through the ages and during the time of Christ when He chose Paul as a chosen vessel to go unto the Gentiles and preach the good news of the kingdom of God. There will no longer be just a remnant of the Gentiles becoming a part of the household of God. Jesus stated, "Also I have other sheep which are not from this pen; I need to bring them, and they will hear my voice; and there will be one flock, one shepherd" (John 10:16, cjb). The Gentiles are those sheep. The pen/fold is His house and the one shepherd is Christ. Read on and you will see the continual formation of the house that Christ built for His growing family.

As a result of the pharaoh not heeding God's warnings, every firstborn died the night the death angel passed over Egypt. Great mourning was heard throughout the land of Egypt. Only the houses with the blood on the frame of the door were passed over. God will do what He says he will do and the nations will know that He alone is God.

The children of Israel are definitely beginning a new life. Afterward, the pharaoh and all of Egypt pretty much demanded the Hebrew children to leave. And just as the Lord had warned them, they were dressed and ready to flee immediately. When they departed, Moses remembered Joseph's request to carry his bones from Egypt and he left with Joseph's bones. "God will certainly remember you; and you are to carry my bones up with you, away from here" (Exodus 13:19, CJB). God guided and protected His people with a pillar of cloud by day and a pillar of fire by night.

For God to receive glory, the pharaoh's heart was hardened and he and his army pursued after the Hebrew children. For their exodus across the Red Sea, God moved the pillar of cloud behind the Hebrew children and the pillar of fire before them to give them light during the night. All through the night, God used a strong wind to part the waters and dry the ground. The pharaoh's army pursued after them in darkness, and just before dawn, the waters came together and drowned all of the pharaoh's army. The Hebrew children would believe in the Lord God and in Moses, and the Egyptians would surely know that God was who He said He was—Lord of all.

Even though they had escaped from the Egyptian army and were safe on the other side of the Red Sea, their troubles were not over. They begin complaining because there was a lack of food and water. They also fought the tribes who were settled in the land they were traveling on. Through all their grumbling, complaining and worshiping idols, God still cared for them and was with them.

News of what God had done for the Hebrew children traveled far and wide. When they were in the land of the Amalek's and after a great battle with them, Jethro, the priest of Midian and Moses's father-in-law, heard about the way God delivered and protected him and the Hebrew children from the pharaoh and his army. Jethro had returned Moses's wife and children to him. Jethro proclaimed, "Blessed be *ADONAI*, who has rescued you from the Egyptians and from Pharaoh… Now I know that *ADONAI* is greater than all other gods." (Exodus 18:10, 11, cjb). Soon after sharing a meal with Moses and his leaders, Jethro returned to his country.[1]

After being in the desert for three months, they arrived at the Mt. Sinai Desert. Moses climbed the mountain and God spoke to him. "Here is what you have to say to the household of Ya'akov (Jacob)." Through Moses God reminded the household of Jacob how He had been with them and delivered them from their oppressor. How He carried them on "eagles' wings" and brought them to

---

1 Jethro was a Gentile in which case Moses's sons were part Hebrew and part Gentile—known as Samaritans during the time of Jesus.

Himself. The message continues, "Now if you will pay careful attention to what I say and keep my covenant, then you will be my own treasure from among all the peoples, for all the earth is mine; and you will be a kingdom of *cohanim* (priests) for me, a nation set apart" (Exodus 19:5–6a, CJB). Moses came down from the mountain and presented to the people what God had said. In unison, the children of Israel said, "Everything *ADONAI* has said, we will do."

The God of Abraham, Isaac, and Jacob on the third day visited His household near the base of the mountain. The thunder, lightning, and thick cloud on the mountain, plus the shofar blast being so loud, the people trembled with fear. God spoke to Moses and asked him to come to Him on the mountain; the remainder of His children stayed behind at a distance. After Moses returned to the foot of the mountain and warned the people not to force their way onto the mountain, God then spoke to His people the Ten Commandments that they were to keep. They too would soon find out that nothing was to be added that was man-initiated, including building the Ark of the Covenant and the tent of meeting. All would be God-instructed and come from the earth or stone that had not been cut. This is a reminder that only God can build His house—His house for His household (His family).

Moses and Joshua went back up into the mountain and God proceeded to give the law and commandments of stone to Moses that had been written by Him.[2]

God gave to Moses instructions on how to build the ark of the covenant that would house the *testimony* that God would give him. God also gave Moses instructions on how the movable sanctuary (tent of meeting) that He would dwell in and all the furnishings that would be inside the sanctuary were to be made. He also instructed Moses to call his brother, Aaron, and Aaron's sons out from the people and they were to serve as priests. (See Exodus 25–30) God also gave Moses instructions on artisanry. (See chapter 31) In the meantime, off of the mountain, God saw evil taking place in the camp and He told Moses to return to camp. A golden calf was being built.

With the excuse that Moses was gone too long, the people went to Aaron and ask him to build them a god that would go with them on their journey. Aaron did, God saw, and was angered with His people. Moses pleaded for their lives and returned to camp. Moses told the descendants of Levi, the third son of Jacob, to go to every man's house kill their own kinsman, their own friend, and their own

---

2 Many other rules or commandments from the Lord were given to Moses and presented to His children. (These can be found in Exodus 21–23.)

neighbor. Three thousand souls died that day because of their desire for an idol. And yet, God stated, "Nevertheless, the time for punishment will come; and then I will punish them for their sin" (Exodus 32:34b, cjb). God also struck them with a plague and that generation died in the wilderness never to enjoy the Promised Land.

After the construction of the tent of meeting, Moses and his minister Joshua would meet with the Lord there. On occasion, Joshua would remain in the tent. I believe God was grooming the next leader, Joshua, for His people. The Hebrew children would need a new leader after Moses's death. But until Moses's death, he was God's vessel to lead His children. And too, the tent of meeting was set up for anyone who wanted to meet with the Lord.

God called Moses to meet him once again on Mt. Sinai. Moses also took a new stone for God to write His commandments on since he had smashed the first stone, when he saw the corruption that was taking place off the mountain: the people worshiping an idol. If you think about it, every household has rules they are to abide by; and if they are not obeyed, there are consequences. So it is in the house of God; the household is accountable for their sins.

Because of God's jealously, He warned Moses: "Do not make a covenant with the people living in the land. It will cause you to go astray after their gods and sacrifice to their gods. Then they will invite you to join them in eating their sacrifices, and you will take their daughters as wives for your sons. Their daughters will prostitute themselves to their own gods and make your sons do the same" (Exodus 34:15, 16, cjb). It has not changed today, "since *ADONAI* – whose very name is Jealous – is a jealous God" (Exodus 34:14b, cjb). "Therefore *Adonai ELOHIM* says this: 'Now I will restore the fortunes of Ya'akov and have compassion on the entire house of Isra'el, and I will be jealous for my holy name" (Ezekiel 39:25, cjb).

Wherever the children of God camped, the priests would pitch the tent of meeting or sanctuary on the outside of the camp on the first day of every month. Every item that was made for the tent, such as the covering, the sockets, the crossbars, posts, the ark of the covenant, the menorah, the bread, etc. was to be placed in their appropriate place that God had instructed. A cloud would cover the tent of meeting and the glory of God would enter it and no one could enter. When the cloud departed from over the meeting place, then the people could move on. When this tent of meeting was constructed and set up, the glory of God would fill it and not even Moses could enter. At other times, the tent of meeting was placed outside the camp where the people could go and consult with the Lord, as the cloud rested over the meeting place, but when Moses entered the tent a cloud would cover it and the people would lay prostrate at their tent door. A cloud would cover the sanctuary by day and a fire in the midst of the cloud by night so the Hebrew children could see it whenever it was set up.

There was a point in time in their travels that they were numbered (counted). Each tribe or clan leader from the eleven of the twelve tribes was to count their family members. They were to record the names of the men twenty years and older (military age) and take a number of the remaining family members from each family in every tribe or clan. With there being eleven tribes with menfolk over the age of twenty, the total was 603,550.

The Levites were not counted. They had been appointed as priests over the tabernacle. They were in charge of everything connected to the tabernacle. They were the ones chosen to carry the tabernacle and all the equipment that went with the tabernacle and everything that was to be placed inside the tabernacle when it was set up. Not only was the firstborn of every human and animal given to the Lord but also the Levite men represented the firstborn of every Egyptian male that was killed when the death angel passed over the Hebrew children. The Lord ordered the sons of Levi to serve Aaron and his sons. Aaron and his sons were the priests in the sanctuary, the meeting place for God's household (See Numbers 3:12, 13, cjb). "When Pharaoh was unwilling to let us go, *ADONAI* killed all the firstborn males in the land of Egypt, both the firstborn of humans and the firstborn of animals. This is why I sacrifice to *ADONAI* any male that is first from the womb of an animal, but all the firstborn of my sons I redeem" (Exodus 13:15, cjb). Today when a Christian couple has children, they offer (dedicate) them to the Lord. Thank God for grace, it is not only the firstborn.

"For in union with the Messiah, you are all children of God through the trusting faithfulness; because as many of you as were immersed into the Messiah have clothed yourselves with the Messiah, in whom there is neither Jew nor Gentile, neither slave nor freeman, neither male nor female; for in union with the Messiah Yeshua, you are all one. If you belong to the Messiah, you are seed of Avraham and heirs according to the promise" (Galatians 3:26–29, cjb). This Scripture is speaking of the household of faith, for the house that Christ built. He completed the foundation, not only with the prophets but also with His apostles, with Himself being the Chief Cornerstone; and from the New Testament era on He is just adding to His family. That is the main reason why the gates of hell will not hinder its completion. He will complete in us what He started before the foundation of the world.

Be sure to know the enemy is trying to kill, steal, and destroy God's family, but by the grace of God, His family will never be destroyed. Many have given their lives for Christ's sake, and I fear that many more will before His return, but His house will stand regardless. Just think when He returns, all His children will be united in His house when He sets it up anew in the New Jerusalem. Until then, His children still need a meeting place, a sanctuary for His ministers to teach and instruct. There are several meeting places throughout the land, and they are all considered the household of faith, God's children—the "Messiah's community" which is called church, synagogue, temple. Shall we continue with our heritage?

Regardless how rebellious the children of Israel were, God still loved them and provided their needs. However because of their disobedience, they wandered in the wilderness for forty years, and Joshua was the one who led them across the Jordan River into the Promise Land. Reason being, Moses disobeyed God on an occasion when he and Aaron "broke faith with me there among the people of Isra'el at the M'rivat-Kadesh (Meribah-Kadesh Spring), in the Tzin Desert (wilderness of Zin); you failed to demonstrate my holiness there among the people of Isra'el" (Deuteronomy 32:51, CJB). Thus, Moses and Aaron forfeited their right to enter the Promise Land. Nonetheless, God told Moses to go up into Mt. Nebo and he was allowed to look over into the land; then he died, and God buried him. Aaron never got to see the Promise Land. God still yet today demands obedience from His leaders who are placed over His children as well as obedience from His children.

A portion of the song that God commanded Moses to teach His children is "You foolish people, so lacking in wisdom, is this how you repay *ADONAI*? He is your father, who made you his! It was he who formed and prepared you…! You ignored the Rock who fathered you, you forgot God, who gave you birth" (Deuteronomy 32:6, 18, CJB). After Moses taught the children of Israel this song, Moses told them, "This is not a trivial matter for you" and still rings true today. This is not a trivial matter for us to play house with God's household—His family. He is our Father, and He also gave us "birth" through Christ.

Haven't I ordered you, "Be strong, be bold"? So don't be afraid or downhearted, because ADONAI your God is with you wherever you go.

—Joshua 1:9, CJB

7

A New Leader

God commissioned Joshua, a type of Christ, to lead His people across the Jordan River into the land that was covenanted to His people. God gave Joshua assurance that He would go with him. Joshua's first action was sending two men to spy out the land and the city of Jericho. In Jericho, the two men stayed in Rahab's house.[1]

Rahab and her household were to be spared if she did not reveal the two men and their plan. Rahab's family consisted of her father's family, mother, brothers, and sisters

---

1   It is interesting that there is going to be an addition added to the family of God from Jericho (a Gentile woman and her household or family). We know her as Rahab, the harlot, but she was a heroine to the people of God. A descendant of Judah married Rahab whose son, three generations later, was Jesse, the father of King David.

and all that were theirs. The command was that her entire family would be spared if they all were in her house when Joshua and his army invaded Jericho.

The men returned to Joshua with their report and they proceeded to cross the Jordan River. Once again, waters were parted for the children of God to cross. Upon crossing, twelve stones were gathered from the middle of the riverbed, representing the twelve tribes of Israel, and they were placed in their first camp, known as Gilgal, after they crossed the Jordan River. This would be a memorial for an everlasting reminder how God delivered them into the Promise Land. Joshua also placed twelve stones in the Jordan River itself where the priests carrying the ark of the covenant stood.

The first thing that God told Joshua to do, after they made camp, was to make sharp knives and circumcise all the males. Those who had wondered in the wilderness for forty years were dead because of their rebellion, and those who crossed the Jordan River with Joshua, besides Caleb, were younger, and they had not been circumcised during the wilderness wonderings. Circumcision was a sign of their perpetual covenant with God that He had made with Abraham, Isaac, and Jacob. God is a promise-keeping God.

Sometime afterward, Joshua was also approached by God, as Moses was, and was told to remove his sandals off his feet because he was standing on holy ground. The particular one who approached Joshua stated that He was "the commander of *ADONAI's* army." Joshua immediately fell on his face before Him and worshiped. (See Joshua 5:13–15, cjb).

After the men were healed from their circumcision, Joshua instructed them how they were going to take the city of Jericho. All instructions were carried out as commanded and the walls of Jericho fell, and Israel remembers Rahab and saves her and her household. According to the Jewish law, anyone who became a part of their family, with the exception that the men had to be circumcised, was added as family. Rahab and her family became a part of God's family because of her faith in their God whom she acknowledged as "God in heaven above and on the earth below."

God loves families. He is such a relational God. He desires relationships. This truly is the house that Christ built—a house where we are brothers and sisters through the Body of Christ, who sits at the right hand of the Father in the kingdom of God. Through Christ we are made one unit—a family. It is not about which church Christ built, but it is about a house that Christ built for His family that He is gathering from all four corners of the earth. We will see this more as we move along.

As with Moses, things did not go as smoothly as Joshua would have liked. Everything and everyone was to be destroyed in Jericho with the exception of "all the silver and gold, and all the brass and iron utensils which was to be separated for *ADONAI* and added to the treasury of *ADONAI*" (Joshua 6:19, CJB). But someone kept some of the things that were to be destroyed and God's anger was kindled against His household; and as a result, in their next battle, some of their soldiers were killed. The remainder of the three thousand soldiers was chased away.

Joshua pleaded with God wanting to know why the battle had been lost! God revealed to him that there was sin in the camp. Someone had stolen items that were to be destroyed. After following God's instructions to find out who the thief was, Achan, of the Tribe of Judah, confessed. He and everything and everyone who belonged to him was stoned and then burned to ashes, and then stones were piled over them. God's anger was appeased, and Ai was given to Joshua. At Jericho, God's orders were to kill the king, the men, women, and children, and they were not to take any spoil, with the exception what was going to be added to the treasury.

Based on the strategy that Joshua laid out before his thirty thousand men, Ai was burned to the ground and all were killed, and the spoils from Ai were kept. The first thing that Joshua did after their victory was to build an altar according to the instructions in the Torah of Moses, and a peace offering sacrificed to God. Joshua then stood before all the people of God and the foreigners who lived among them and read the entire Torah that Moses had written.

There were a series of battles that God lead them through victoriously. Actually, including Jericho, there were thirty-one kings that Joshua and his people defeated, but yet there was still land to possess. Joshua was to divide the possessed land by lots to the children of Israel as an inheritance only to nine and one-half tribes. Moses had already given the Reubenites and the Gadites their inheritance east of Jordan. The Levites' inheritance was "the offerings made by fire for *ADONAI* the God of Israel" as instructed by God.

Caleb also reminded Joshua about the land that Moses promised him when he and Joshua were sent from Kadesh-barnea with ten other men to spy out the land. When the twelve spies had returned, only Joshua and Caleb told Moses that they could take the land, but the remaining ten spies disagreed with the report. Thus the land was given to Caleb because he "followed *ADONAI* the God of Isra'el completely."

The family of God received their inheritance as promised from their heavenly Father. (See Joshua 13–22 for the entire distribution of the inheritances and cities.) There still was much land to possess at this time, but Joshua was nearing his end. At the age of 110, he reminded the people of God of all their deliverances up until that day— their ancestors delivered out of Egypt, their deliverances from many enemies, and enjoying the land that they were living on. He also charged them to wholly serve the Lord. (See chapters 23 and 24).

Their inheritance had been distributed and now it was time to possess the land with the promise that God would be with them. As brothers should, they aided one another in the battles with the tribes they were warring with to possess the land. After the death of Joshua, the elders, and those who inherited the lands died, the generation that followed did not serve the Lord. They did what was right in their own eyes. As punishment, the tribes who were not driven out of the Promise Land became the Hebrew children's enemies. They intermingled and married outside their household of faith. Also, the young nation learned war because of those who God did not drive out from among them. In the end, the Hebrew children served the nation's gods who surrounded them; a warning that God had given to Moses not to do.

God's love and covenant for His people was everlasting and when they cried out to Him for help, God would rise up an individual who would become their judge and prophet or prophetess and lead them. After the death of each judge, they would again commit evil in the sight of the Lord, and, as a result, He would turn them over to a king who would war against them.

Othniel, Caleb's younger brother, was the first judge who delivered the children of Israel from the hand of their enemies. Under Deborah's leadership, the fourth judge, and after a victorious battle against Jabin, king of Canaan, there was peace. Forty years under her reign as judge and prophetess, the children of God enjoyed peace.

Following the death of Deborah, once again Israel did evil in the sight of the Lord. God turned them over to the Midianites for seven years until they cried out to Him. So it continued for years and through thirteen judges. The Hebrew children would be repentant and then turn to rebellion as each deliverer God sent to His people died. Following Samson, there was no longer a leader, and the children, as before, did what was right in their own eyes.

He gave some people as emissaries, some as prophets, some as proclaimers of the Good News, and some as shepherds and teachers. Their task is to equip God's people for the work of service that builds the body of the Messiah.

—Ephesians 4:11, 12, CJB

8

Obedience in God's House

Every home ought to have a father. Unfortunately, that is not the case. Many homes are fatherless. There also are many homes that have a father who are not being a real father. However, many have found solace in their heavenly Father. The house of God has a Father who Christ called "Our Father in heaven," and later He said, "Abba," meaning dear father, dad, or even daddy. Through Christ we can have an intimate relation with our heavenly Father. From the children of God, the Lord appointed the Tribe of Levi as priests and they were to adhere to God as Father. The Lord gave Moses instructions on everything that the priests were to do. They were to go before the Father before anything new was to be done.

The Tribe of Levi was set apart to serve the Lord in the tent of meeting or tabernacle, a place established for the children of God to go before the Lord. The people were to bring their sacrifices to the tent of meeting and present them before the Lord and the priests, whether it was a sin offering, a peace offering, or a wave offering. The Levites were "taken from among the people of Isra'el in lieu of every firstborn male that is first from the womb among the people of Isra'el: the L'vi'im are to be mine" (Numbers 3:12, CJB).[1]

Their responsibilities could be strenuous at times. They were the ones who were to carry the tent of meeting and every part of it. They were to set it up with everything in its proper place, when they were not traveling, for the children of God to go to commune with the Lord.

There has to be order and obedience in any house. The teaching and the understanding of the ways of God are given to His leaders for the "perfecting of the saints." It is done through congregational gatherings. Just as the responsibilities of the Father are important for a family to thrive spiritually, so are the responsibilities of leadership in God's house for the family of God to thrive spiritually. The Old Testament priesthood is an example of obedience and unfortunately disobedience as given in the following examples. Let us look at these examples of disobedience as lessons.

---

1   This did not prevent all the firstborns of Israel from being redeemed by God. (See Numbers 3:40–51, CJB).

Two of Aaron's sons were slain by the Lord because they offered strange fire before the Lord. They failed to ask the Lord for directions in adding incense to a censer with fire in it and offering it before the Lord; as a result, they were slain. Incense was brought before the Lord but not in the manner it was done. Instructions were given to Moses to build an altar specifically to burn incense on. The priests were to burn it when the lamps were prepared and when the lamps were lit at dark. That was to be "the regular burning of incense before *ADONAI* through all your generations. You are not to offer unauthorized incense on it" (See Exodus 30:1–9, CJB). They did something new by adding incense to the censer that had fire; thus they depended on their own wisdom. Therefore, it was just a "show of wisdom and humility" which resulted in "strange fire" before the Lord (See Leviticus 10:1).

Many times, leaders act before asking God for direction, and they and God's children suffer the consequence. Still yet today, it is serious business to stand before the children of God and proclaim His Word. Many generations of believers have been led astray because leaders did not ask for divine revelation of His written Word. We know this by the virtual thousands of different denominations or belief systems that are throughout our world today. Of course, we also know that individuals like to interpret Scriptures and start their own organizations which lead many astray.

As a result, many different interpretations of Scripture are spoken and actually thousands do not know who or what to believe. The crux of the matter, only God can change this dilemma that Christendom is faced with; and as long as Christ is their Savior that big problem belongs to Him. How He will handle it is none of our business.

We will look at a priest and his sons—particularly Eli and his sons, Hophni and Phinehas. Eli was growing old and his two sons were partaking in the priesthood but not with pure hearts. When the children of God came to offer a sacrifice to the Lord, the priest's servant came and took a portion of the meat for himself from everyone who came to the tent of meeting. And also before an individual would burn the fat, the priest's servant would threaten to take a portion by force if he would not give him a portion to roast prior to it being burnt. In other words, the priests were taking a large quantity of the sacrifices for themselves. This was not pleasing to the Lord.

The tribe of Levites lost much of their privileges because of Eli and his sons. God told them they would all die young and they would beg to be a priest so that they would have food to eat (See 1 Samuel 2). Eli's sons had so profaned the tent of meeting that a number of people quit going to offer their sacrifices. As a result, the sons of Eli died in battle, and the ark of God was taken; and upon hearing the results of the ark of God, Eli fell off his seat backward, broke his neck, and died.

God's judgment was totally fulfilled on the priesthood during the reign of King Solomon, when King Solomon expelled Abiathar from his priestly duties. Abiathar had assisted in setting Solomon's brother up as king while David was still king. King Solomon dealt with the three main characters in that escapade. His brother, Adonijah, who wanted the throne was eventually slain; Joab, captain of King David's army, was slain; and Abiathar, the priest, was made to leave and return to his own fields thus fulfilling prophecy against Eli's descendants (See 1 Kings 2:26, 27).

Christ also confronted evildoers in the temple. He expelled money changers and those who sold doves who were taking advantage of His people when they came to the temple during Passover. The money changers were also disrupting the court of Gentiles which was in the temple. Jesus was angered and braided a whip and ran them out the temple, and overturned the money changers' tables. He said, "It has been written, 'My house will be called a house of prayer.' But you are making it into a den of robbers" (Matthew 21:13, CJB). Jesus was quoting from the writings of the prophet Isaiah. This was a place where God's household was to gather and pray and worship the Lord, but they were using it to benefit themselves. This too was what the priests were doing under the leadership of Eli. They were taking advantage of God's family, to benefit themselves, when the people went to the tent of meeting to offer their sacrifice to the Lord.

*For certain individuals, the ones written about long
ago as being meant for this condemnation, have
wormed their way in – ungodly people who pervert
God's grace into a license for debauchery and disown
our only Master and Lord, Yeshua the Messiah.*

—Jude 4, CJB

9

God's House

God's house of worship was a place intended for His children to go and commune with Him. His presence or glory resided in His house. It was not to be profaned in any way.

Thus it is today. All God's children who are of the seed of Abraham through Jesus Christ; regardless of what denomination, has a meeting place to meet with their Lord and Savior to offer themselves as a living sacrifice, and to worship Him. Of course we also know we can meet with our heavenly Father anytime/anyplace, but as a community of believers we come together in a designated place which is called today "Church," but in the days of wondering it was called "tent of meeting or tabernacle" and in the New Testament, temple or "Messianic community or congregation."

The important thing to remember is that the gates of hell will not destroy what Christ builds. Jesus said, "I also tell you this: you are Kefa (Peter)," [which means 'Rock,'] "and on this rock I will build my Community, and the gates of Sh'ol (hell) will not overcome it" (Matthew 16:18, CJB). Since Christ is the Rock, His community is built on Him and He was adding to His house that He started generations before. And He was very adamant when He stated that the gates of hell will not overcome it.[1]

History has proven that Satan has tried to destroy faithful ones. They have been tortured in many different ways. If one would read *Foxe's Book of Martyrs* one would

---

1   There is a difference between the rock that Christ called Peter and the rock He referred to as Himself. In Greek, the name Peter means a (piece of) rock—Petros. The rock that Christ is considered is Petra a (mass of) rock. Not only is the house or community that Christ built referred to in the New Testament but also in the Old Testament. Paul stated, "For, brothers I don't want you to miss the significance of what happened to our fathers. All of them were guided by the pillar of cloud, and they all passed through the sea, and in connection with the cloud and with the sea they all immersed themselves into Moshe, also they all ate the same food from the Spirit, and they all drank the same drink from the Spirit—for they drank from a Spirit-sent Rock which followed them, and that Rock was the Messiah" (1 Corinthians 10:1, CJB).

understand the length that the evil one went and is still going today to destroy God's community of believers—Christ's household. But hallelujah he will fail, and Christ is the Victor.

If all believers would consider themselves part of a family, the family of God, is it possible there would be less schism in the Body of Christ. Wouldn't we be less likely to condemn one another? We may not all agree on things but tell me a household in the natural that sees eye to eye on everything; but yet the love is there. When one hurts, they all hurt; when one falls, they all pull together to try to restore the relationship. This is the way it should be in the Body of Christ.

Before we move on, I want to take you to Isaiah 8:23(9:1)–9:2(3), CJB. God's people had failed Him tremendously to the point that the Assyrian army was permitted to invade Israel. However, a prophecy was spoken that stated that a "great light" would come. We see in verse 8:23b(9:1) God will honor His people "beyond the Yarden (Jordan), Galil-of-the-*Goyim* (Galilee of the nations meaning Gentiles, or non-Jews)." It also speaks of the "people (the Jews) living in darkness who have seen a great light" even to the extent that those (Gentiles), "living in the land that lies in the shadow of death, light has dawned" (See verse 2[3], CJB). It is followed with, "You (the Jews) have enlarged the nation (Abraham's seed, the Jewish people, God's household) and increased their (the Gentiles) joy; they rejoice in your presence as if rejoicing at harvest time, the way men rejoice when dividing up the spoil" (Isaiah 9:3, cjb).

This prophecy foretold speaks of the Jews who were living in darkness; and the Gentiles, who lived in the shadow of death. All, Jews and Gentiles, who believed in the coming great Light would be blessed as part of Abraham's inheritance, because the Gentiles would be grafted into the family of God—His household; and *all* would be part of the house that Christ built.

I believe we cannot understand the New Testament in its entirety until we grasp the Old Testament and its prophecies being fulfilled. Of course, we understand that the prophecy in Isaiah 8:23 (9:1)–9:2 (3) was fulfilled in Matthew when Christ stated right before He healed the blind man, "While I am in the world, I am the light of the world" (John 9:5, cjb).

The door was opened to the Gentiles when God made it plain to Peter when He told him in a dream, "Stop treating as unclean what God has made clean" (Acts 10:15, cjb). And of course, God saw Cornelius's (a Gentile) faith and sent Peter to him to witness to him and his household, and to baptize them. When Peter explained to the Jewish believers in Jerusalem what had taken place, they praised God and said, "This means that God has enabled the *Goyim* (Gentiles) as well to do *t'shuvah* (repentance) and have life"

(Acts 11:18b, cjb). It would no longer be a few Gentiles along the way to receive the Good News of Christ, but Salvation was opened to the Gentile nation as well as the Jewish nation.

Let us look back on history to understand more about God's household. During the period of the judges and the reign of the kings, God would turn Israel over to various nations which caused them to cry out to Him, to forsake their backslidden ways, and to return to the God of Abraham, Isaac, and Jacob. In the latter days of Samuel, they no longer wanted theocratic government, they wanted a king to rule them. The priests had failed God in maintaining the written word of God through Moses. Nonetheless, there were those who maintained their integrity and believed in God. We shall look at the kings that God placed over His people.

ADONAI said to Sh'mu'el (Samuel), "Listen to the people, to everything they say to you; for it is not you they are rejecting; they are rejecting me; they don't want me to be king over them."

—1 Samuel 8:7, cJB

10

Kings

After Eli and his sons, the priest, Samuel, tried to keep the children of Israel following in the ways of Abraham, Isaac, and Jacob. He saw the wickedness of the priests even in the tent of meeting—sanctuary, where the people were to come and offer their sacrifices to God. Not only did he see the evil from others but also in his own sons. The elders also saw the perversion of Samuel's sons and knew that Samuel was old. The elders gathered together, went to Samuel, and ask for a king to judge them like the nations surrounding them. Even though Samuel told them that they would be as servants to a king, they still desired one. God told Samuel that they were not rejecting him (Samuel) but they were rejecting His theocratic government and let them have what they wanted. Unfortunately the people saw that the priests were corrupt and they failed to trust God to rise up a leader for them. They wanted a king as the surrounding nations had.

God told Samuel to anoint Saul as king. God knew what was going to happen with Saul down the road, but He did not allow what He knew Saul would do in the future to affect His present decision. He is not only in the past; He is in the present, as well as in the tomorrows. We also know that everything that happens on the world stage was/ is pointing to the coming of the Lord Jesus Christ, His advent and His second coming.

> Jonathan Edwards explained in *A History of the Work of Redemption*: God, doubtless, is pursuing some design and carrying on some scheme in the various changes and revolutions which from age to age come to pass in the world. It is most reasonable to suppose that all revolutions, from the beginning of the world to the end of it, are but the various part of the same scheme, all conspiring to bring to pass that great event which the Great Creator and Governor of the world has ultimately in view.5

Saul failed God through the sin of disobedience. As a result, God told Samuel to anoint another: David, a shepherd boy, the son of Jesse from the tribe of Judah. God told Samuel, "Fill your horn with oil, and set out; I will send you to Yishai the Beit-Lachmi (Jesse the Beth-lehemite), because I have chosen myself a king from among his sons" (1 Samuel 16:1b, cjb). Samuel anointed David as king. The "great Light" would come from the household of David. David was a man after God's heart.

A portion of Moses's song in Deuteronomy 31:10 refers to Israel (Jacob) "like the pupil of his (God's) eye." Thus was the prayer of David in Psalms 17:8, when he cried out "Protect me like the pupil of your eye." And God did protect him, not from hardship and family dilemma, but from his enemies, and for the wonderful seed of God (Jesus Christ) through the lineage of David.

Saul's reign brought about disunity among the Hebrew children. However, God's purpose would be fulfilled. His people would be reunited once again. King Saul and his son, Jonathan, were killed in battle, and David was crowned king. Seven years later, he became king over all of Israel, all of God's family.

Unlike families that I mentioned earlier that agree to disagree, there are also families at some point in their relationship have had disagreements and have lasted for years. Some never are resolved, and others come to terms. So it was in David's household. Many issues were never resolved, maybe appeased but never resolved, but God still had a plan for David's household and it is still growing today.

David's desire was to build a temple for the Lord, but because of being a man of war, he was denied the privilege. God told him the following through Nathan the prophet: "Moreover, *ADONAI* tells you that *ADONAI* will make you a house" (2 Samuel 7:11b, cjb). What is this house? It is not the temple because Solomon will build the temple. So what is the house that God will build David? Through his lineage, Christ Jesus, King of kings and Lord of lords, will be born. Christ has set up a kingdom that will have no end; thus, David's house will truly enlarge itself through the bloodline of Christ. But yet Christ never had children! Oh, but yes He did and He is still having children today and it began with Adam. Everyone who accepts His kingship as Lord and Savior enters not only into the royal bloodline of Christ but also of David's. The inheritance of Abraham will become a part of all God's children, Jew and Gentile, to enjoy and David's house is continuing to enlarge.

Nathan proceeds to tell David in verse13 that David's flesh and blood would be the one to build a house for His (God's) name and it would be his son, King Solomon. That house would be the temple where God's children would go to offer sacrifices, and to meet with Him, and where His glory would reside. Nathan continues that his (David's) royal throne would be established forever. The royal throne would be established forever through God's Son, King Jesus. God promised David that He would build David's house and also have His own house. What am I saying? David's house is the family of God extended through Christ, and Christ's house is where He will rule from in the New Jerusalem where His family will be invited to rule and reign.

When King Solomon built the temple, it was a meeting place for God's glory to dwell. "When the *cohanim* (priests) came out of the Holy Place, the cloud filled the house of *ADONAI*, so that, because of the cloud, the *cohanim* could not stand up to perform their service; for the glory of *ADONAI* filled the house of *ADONAI*" (1 Kings 8:10, 11, cjb). God had given the instruction on how to build His house (temple) to King David, and King Solomon was to build His house according to those instructions. We can see David's house enlarging through faith in Christ and Christ's house enlarging through His shed blood. Amazing.

That temple was destroyed. The next temple was built by King Herod but yet, Christ considered it as "My house." (See Mathew 21:13) Nonetheless, this temple would not do for God's glory to dwell in because it had been "made into a den of thieves." Once again in the New Jerusalem, God's glory will dwell in His temple, and we will be able to enter His throne room at any time. We can only enter now through prayer in Jesus's name, but one day, we will see Him face to face as kings and priests.

Who will be kings and priests in the New Jerusalem? This will be discussed in greater length in a following chapter. David was so excited over this prophecy that he went before the Lord, and wanted to know who was he that God would do such a marvelous work for, that his dynasty would continue on. We, as Christians, truly are a continuation of

David's dynasty. David said, "Who can be compared with your people, with Isra'el? What other nation on earth did God set out to redeem and make into a people for himself" (2 Samuel 7: 23a, CJB)? David proclaimed God's promise to him, "I will build you a house" (verse 27). (Read the entire account in 2 Samuel 11-27, KJV or CJB) As a Christian, we are a part of David's dynasty, the family of God.

David reigned forty years, and from his prayer mentioned in chapter 7, he was pleased; at the end of his days knowing God was building his dynasty—his house to last forever. He may not have understood how it would happen, but he believed and accepted what the Lord said through Nathan the prophet. And here we are today, through Christ Jesus, we are a part of his household and longing to be a part of God's house. But the amazing thing is:, we are through Jesus Christ. We, as children of God, are already a part of the New Jerusalem through the shed blood of Christ; we are just waiting until the day we will forever be with the Lord. The seed of David's dynasty was carried down generations through his son Nathan to Mary, the mother of Jesus. (Read Luke 3:31) Joseph's lineage was through Solomon, son of David.

Solomon was crowned king before King David's death in order to keep Adonijah, his half brother, from being set up as king. Nonetheless, Solomon ended his life with a prophecy against him and his son who would rule and reign after him. The throne would be taken away from the house of Solomon because of his marriages to women outside of His faith and permitting idol worship. However, Solomon was a good king in the beginning. He truly did build a temple for the presence of the Lord, and God's glory came down and filled the temple on the day of dedication to the extent that the priests were unable to minister.

We see two things taking place: David's dynasty will never end (through Christ Jesus) and the temple was built for God's presence to dwell in on this earth. So where is God's temple today? Isaiah wrote the Lord's words as such: "Heaven is my throne," says *ADONAI*, "and the earth is my footstool. What kind of house could you build for me? What sort of place could you devise for my rest? Didn't I myself make all these things? This is how they all came to be" (Isaiah 66:1, 2a). The tent of meeting was desecrated with Eli's sons. Solomon's temple where God dwelt was destroyed by Nebuchadnezzar II after the Siege of Jerusalem in 587 BC. So where would God's spirit dwell on earth today? God's spirit would dwell on earth today in His children through Christ Jesus. At the end of the Gentile world system, all God's children will be welcomed home and "dwell in the house of the Lord forever." But in the meantime, His children are being built up into Jesus Christ as a spiritual temple. This will become clearer as we proceed with God's building plan.

This is not a new thing, it started way back when, but for generations, God lacked a temple to dwell in. His family did not quit growing, but His glory ceased having a place on earth until His Son came. Christ was/is the Light of the world—we have established that. When He left, He charged His children to be His light in the world. He built His house a long time ago, but there was no temple that was not corrupt where His children could go to worship in spirit and in truth and receive guidance or His word. However, there was a flicker of light shining down through the ages during the reformation, the great awakening and other times throughout history. There also were times of silence from our Father.

We are His temple, and as His temple go and minister to whoever will listen. "Don't you know that you people are God's temple and that God's Spirit lives in you? So if anyone destroys God's temple, God will destroy him. For God's temple is holy, and you yourselves are that temple" (1 Corinthians 3:16, 17, CJB). Paul quotes a portion of Leviticus 26:12: "For we are the temple of the living God— as God said, I will house myself in them.... And I will walk among you. I will be their God, and they will be my people." Paul continues with "Therefore *ADONAI* says, Go out from their midst; separate yourselves; don't even touch what is unclean. Then I myself will receive you. In fact, I will be your Father, and you will be my sons and daughters, says *ADONAI-Tzva'ot* (the Lord of Host)" (2 Corinthians 6:16–18, cjb). Sons and daughters is a beautiful depiction of family. We are His temple that God dwells in. No one had a hand in building us; we are from His book of design. He chose us and has fashioned us pleasing to Himself. His glory through Christ rests in us. Let us once again return to the kings.

Several kings followed King Solomon, but the kingdom was divided. Kings failed to obey God's commandments in every way conceivable. Josiah, was made king at the age of eight years. He loved God, but knew nothing of the laws of God. The Scriptures call him a good king who walked in the way of David his father. After eighteen years of being king; he asked his scribe to gather the silver from the temple which the people had given for repairing the damaged places in the temple. It was during the time that the scroll was found that Josiah realized the people were not obeying God's commandments, and that the Lord could be angry with His people. When he heard the Words of the Lord being read to him, he tore his clothes, and was fearful. He asked the priest to consult with the Lord to find out how strong was God's wrath toward them. Just thinking, what had the priests been doing all those years?

The priest took the scrolls to Huldah, the prophetess, and she sent word to the king that he would be spared the wrath of God that would come upon His people because of their disobedience. As a result of the words from the Lord, King Josiah went into the house of the Lord and read "all the words of the book of the covenant" to all the men of Jerusalem and of Judah. The king then stood before the people and he made a covenant with the Lord that he would live following the Lord's commandments, instructions, and regulations with all his being. The temple was cleansed of all the things that were offensive to the Lord. The remainder of the thirty-one years that Josiah reigned, he followed wholehearted after the Lord. The family of God was once again united and living under the protection of their heavenly Father.

In memory of King Josiah, the following words would be written of him. "No previous king was like him; because he turned to *ADONAI* with all his heart, with all his being and with all his power, in accordance with all the Torah of Moshe; nor did any king like him arise afterwards" (2 Kings 23:25, CJB). But because of the years of God's leaders and people not keeping His commandments, His anger burned against Judah. They would pay dearly for their disobedience. The kings following Josiah experienced servitude under various nations and kings and finally Jerusalem was taken by their enemies.

However, God's covenant would not be forgotten. His covenant with Abraham, Isaac, Jacob, and David was a perpetual covenant. Even though the tribes of Israel were divided, He still loved His children. Therefore, a new covenant was prophesied by Jeremiah and fulfilled through Christ Jesus. So much is brought out in the New Testament that relates to God's covenant with His people, His household. We will look at the New Testament prophecies of the coming of Christ that will take us back to the Old Testament.

But to the Son, he says, "Your throne, O God, will last forever and ever; you rule your Kingdom with a scepter of equity."

—Hebrews 1:8, cjb

11

Prophecies Foretold
of Christ the Messiah

Many prophecies are foretold of the coming Messiah. I will begin with the prophecy told by a person who did not know God personally, but God knew him. The son of Zippor, Balak, saw how Israel was growing, not only numerically, but also in conquering land. Of course, he doesn't realize that this was a covenant that God made with Abraham and his seed concerning the land promised to them. Nonetheless, he approaches Balaam, a false teacher, and asked him to curse Israel. God would not permit such a thing against His children. Instead, Balaam prophesied over Israel and spoke of a scepter that would rise from Israel to crush the corners of Moab, God's enemies, and destroy all the descendants of Seth (those sons and daughters who failed to follow wholeheartedly after the commandments of God). "I see him, but not now; I behold him, but not soon—-a star will step forth from Ya'akov, a scepter will arise from Isra'el, to crush the corners of Mo'av (the descendants of Lot and his firstborn daughter) and destroy all descendants of Shet" (Numbers 24:17, CJB). God will use whom He chooses to accomplish His will in heaven and in earth even if He has to use a heathen.

Father God gave all power to His Son in earth, in heaven, and even in hell. Christ was foretold in Genesis when Adam and Eve disobeyed God and all mankind fell into sin. "I will put animosity between you and the woman, and between your descendant and her descendant; he will bruise your head, and you will bruise his heel" (Genesis 3:15, CJB). Christ was going to build His family and His enemy would hinder, but ultimately, Christ will be the Victor over death, hell, and the grave.

Because of sin and disobedience, God was not going to forsake His family. "Can a woman forget her child at the breast, not show pity on the child from her womb? Even if these were to forget, I would not forget you. I have engraved you on the palms of my hands, your walls are always before me" (Isaiah 49:15, 16, CJB). Isaiah foretold of His coming in 7:14, CJB: "Therefore *Adonai* himself will give you people a sign: the young woman (the virgin) will become pregnant, bear a son and name him 'Immanu El [God is with us]."

To prevent me from reinventing the wheel so to speak below are many promises, provided by Walter C. Kaiser Jr.

in the Nov 2006 issue of *Decision Magazine*. Those I have already mentioned will not be repeated.

> He would come from the seed/offspring of Abraham and would bless all the nations on earth (Genesis 12:3).

> He would be a "prophet like Moses" to whom God said we must listen (Deuteronomy 18:15).

> He would be born in Bethlehem of Judah (Micah 5:2).

> He would have a throne, a kingdom and a dynasty, or house, starting with King David, that will last forever (2 Samuel 7:16).

> He would be called "Wonderful Counselor," "Mighty God," "Everlasting Father," "Prince of Peace," and would possess an everlasting kingdom (Isaiah 9:6-7).

> He would ride into Jerusalem on a donkey, righteous and having salvation, coming with gentleness (Zechariah 9:9-10).

> He would be pierced for our transgression and crushed for our iniquities (Isaiah 53:5).

> He would die among the wicked ones but be buried with the rich (Isaiah 53:9).

He would be resurrected from the grave, for God would not allow His Holy One to suffer decay (Psalm 16:10).

He would come again from the clouds of heaven as the Son of Man (Daniel 7:13-14).

He would be the "Sun of Righteousness" for all who revere Him and look for His coming again (Malachi 4:2).

He is the One whom Israel will one day recognize as the One they pierced, causing bitter grief (Zechariah 12:10).

She gave birth to a son, a male child, the one who will rule all the nations with a staff of iron. But her child was snatched up to God and his throne; and she fled into the desert, where she has a place prepared by God so that she can be taken care of for 1,260 days.

—Revelation 12:5, 6, CJB

12

Jesus Is Coming Again

The prophecy of Jesus's birth was fulfilled. He was born of a virgin, lived thirty-three years, and gave His life that others might have life. And as prophesied, He is coming again. He will fulfill prophecy foretold of Him from the very beginning of time, as we know time. The Word tells us that Israel surely did give us a Savior. The handmaiden of the Lord who was espoused to Joseph was visited by an angel, and the angel told her that she would conceive by the Holy Ghost overshadowing her, and she would deliver a son; He would save His people from their sins. Mary and Joseph both are from the lineage of King David.[1] God was going to fulfill the promise He made to David generations before that He (God) would build David a house. The house was

---

1   Mary through the lineage of David's son Nathan, and Joseph through the lineage of Solomon.

about to take shape through Mary, and as a result peoples from every tribe, tongue, and nation would become a part of David's dynasty and Christ's house. "She will give birth to a son, and you are to name him Yeshua, [which means '*ADONAI* saves,'] because he will save his people from their sins. All this happened in order to fulfill what *ADONAI* had said through the prophet, 'The virgin will conceive and bear a son, and they will call him 'Immanu El (Emmanual)'" (Matthew 1:21–23, cjb).

Following the death, burial, and resurrection of Jesus, He returned to His Father and will return again. "So then, after he had spoken to them, the Lord Yeshua was taken up into heaven and sat at the right hand of God" (Mark 16:19, cjb). Jesus said that He would return for His children—His family. "In my Father's house are many places to live. If there weren't, I would have told you; because I am going there to prepare a place for you. Since I am going and preparing a place for you, I will return to take you with me; so that where I am, you may be also" (John 14: 2–3, cjb).

There is a prerequisite to go with Him when He returns: being a part of His household—otherwise left behind to endure God's wrath during the Tribulation. "For God so loved the world that he gave his only and unique Son, so that everyone who trusts in him may have eternal life, instead of being utterly destroyed" (John 3:16, cjb).

"But he was wounded because of our crimes, crushed because of our sins; the disciplining that makes us whole fell on him, and by his bruises (and in fellowship with him) we are healed" (Isaiah 53:5, CJB). His household is in fellowship with Him. "For you have been delivered by grace through trusting, and even this is not your accomplishment but God's gift" (Ephesians 2:8, CJB). "But to as many as did receive him, to those who put their trust in his person and power, he gave the right to become children of God, not because of bloodline, physical impulse or human intention, but because of God" (John 1:12, 13, CJB). This Scripture covers both Jews and Gentiles.

There will be nations of people who make it through the tribulation, living outside the gates, but not permitted to enter because they did not believe in the Messiah. After the tribulation, Scripture says in Matthew 24:30, 31, CJB, "Then the sign of the Son of Man will appear in the sky, all the tribes of the Land will mourn, and they will see the Son of Man coming on the clouds of heaven with tremendous power and glory. He will send out his angels with a great shofar; and they will gather together his chosen people from the four winds, from one end of heaven to the other."

Jews and Gentiles of those that the angels gathered from the four corners of the earth will be rescued from total destruction. They will live in a new Earth and in a New Jerusalem established for all God's children; those who were raptured, those who are His chosen and their sins forgiven that were in the tribulation. "As the Tanakh says, Out of Tziyon (Zion) will come the Redeemer; he will turn away ungodliness from Ya'akov (Jacob or Israel) and this will be my covenant with them, when I take away their sins. With respect to the Good News they are hated for your sake. But with respect to being chosen they are loved for the Patriarchs' sake, for God's free gifts and his calling are irrevocable" (Romans 11:26–29, cjb). Also, there will be those Jews and Gentiles who make it through the tribulation but not permitted inside the gate because they still do not have a pure heart. Those who confessed faith in the Messiah during the tribulation and those who were caught up and met the Lord in the air will live inside the gate. Those who were caught up in the rapture will be kings and priests; they will have taken on a celestial body. Also the Old Testament saints will enjoy reigning with Christ in their homeland.

"I saw no Temple in the city, for *ADONAI*, God of heaven's armies, is its Temple, as is the Lamb. The city has no need for the sun or the moon to shine on it, because God's Sh'khinah (glory) gives it light, and its lamp is the Lamb. The nations will walk by its light, and the kings of the earth will bring their splendor into it. Its gates will never close, they stay open all day because night will not exist there, and the honor and splendor of the nations will be brought into it. Nothing impure may enter it, nor anyone who does shameful things or lies; the only ones who may enter are those whose names are written in the Lamb's Book of Life" (Revelation 21:22–27, CJB). Those who confessed Jesus as the Messiah or Lord during the tribulation their names will be written in the *Lamb's Book of Life*. Those who made it through the tribulation by sheer will, they will live outside the gate because their hearts were not made pure through faith in Christ. After living a thousand years of peace, they will be deceived again by the evil one when he is loosed from his prison for a while; "but the fire came down from heaven and consumed them." The Adversary who had deceived them was hurled into the lake of fire and sulfur, where the beast and the false prophet were, and they will be tormented day and night forever and ever" (Revelation 20:9b, 10, CJB).

Everything written about me in the Torah of Moshe,
the Prophets and the Psalms had to be fulfilled.

—Luke 24:44, CJB

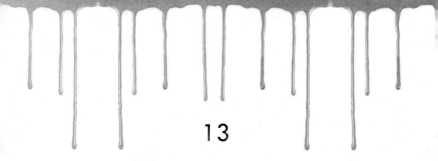

13

Jesus Christ the Messiah: Fulfillment of All Things

Jesus Christ fulfilled everything that was in the law of Moses and in the tent of meeting in the wilderness and also in the temple in Jerusalem. Jesus said to a Torah expert, "You are to love *ADONAI* your God with all your heart and with all your soul and with all your strength. This is the greatest and most important *mitzvah* (commandment). And a second is similar to it, 'You are to love your neighbor as yourself.' All of the *Torah* and the Prophets are dependent on these two *mitzvot* (commandments)" (Matthew 22:37–40, cjb).

The following is His fulfillment as our tabernacle and the remainder is His fulfillment in the tabernacle:

Christ is our tabernacle. Christ is our meeting place where we can commune with the Father. Just as the Hebrew children had a place to go and meet with their Creator, we too have a meeting place. "Here is the whole point of what we have been saying: we do have just such a *cohen gadol* (high priest) as had been described. And he does sit at the right hand of *HaG'dulah* (the Greatness, the Majesty) in heaven. There he serves in the Holy Place, that is, in the true Tent of Meeting, the one erected not by human beings but by *ADONAI*" (Hebrews 8:1, 2, CJB).

Christ is the door or the way into the tabernacle or the very presence of God the Father. Through Christ we can pray, "Our Father in heaven! May your Name be kept holy. May your Kingdom come, your will be done on earth as in heaven" (Matthew 6:9, 10, CJB). The disciples called Christ "the way." Jesus said of Himself, "...I AM the Way – and the Truth and the Life; no one comes to the Father except through me" (John 14:6, CJB). Jesus also stated, "I am the gate (door); if someone enters through me, he will be safe and will go in and out and find pasture" (John 10:9, CJB).

Christ is both the high priest and the sacrificial lamb. We can go to Him as our high priest, our intercessor to the Father, because he was/is the paschal lamb who gave His life for the sins of the world. The descendants of the Levites are no longer considered priests in the kingdom of God. "Moreover, the present *cohanim* (priests) are many in number, because they are prevented by death from continuing in office. But because he lives forever, his position as *cohen* (priest) does not pass on to someone else, and consequently, he is totally able to deliver those who approach God through him;

since he is alive forever and thus forever able to intercede on their behalf" (Hebrews 7:23–25, cjb). "But he was wounded because of our crimes, crushed because of our sins; the disciplining that makes us whole fell on him, and by his bruises we are healed" (Isaiah 53:5, cjb). "So, brothers, we have confidence to use the way into the Holiest Place opened by the blood of Yeshua. He inaugurated it for us as a new and living way through the *parokhet* (veil), by means of his flesh. We also have a great *cohen* (priest) over God's household" (Hebrews 10:19–21, cjb).

Christ is the laver. Aaron and his sons washed their hands and feet in a basin made with bronze (the laver) when they entered the meeting place and approached the altar. (See Exodus 30:17–21) Jesus Christ is our cleansing laver. When we come into the presence of Christ, all of our iniquities are revealed. We see ourselves for who we truly are, a sinner needing a Savior. He is our sanctifier, the cleanser of our sinful human nature. "For both Yeshua, who sets people apart (cleanses) for God and the ones being set apart (cleansed) have a common origin—this is why he is not ashamed to call them brothers" (Hebrews 2:11, cjb). "And the blood of his Son Yeshua purifies us from all sin" (1 John 1:7c, cjb).

Christ is our lampstand (Menorah). He is the Menorah (light) of the world. Without His light (His saving grace) in the world, there would be total chaos. Jesus said, "I am the light of the world; whoever follows me will never walk in darkness but will have the light which gives life" (John 8:12 cjb). In the New Jerusalem there will not be a need for light as we know light because He will be the light. "Night will no longer exist, so they will need neither the light of a lamp nor the light of the sun, because *ADONAI*, God, will shine upon them" (Revelation 22:5, cjb).

Christ is the bread of the present. Jesus said, "I am the Bread of life." "Yeshua said to them, 'Yes, indeed! I tell you it wasn't Moshe who gave you the bread from heaven. But my Father is giving you the genuine bread from heaven; for God's bread is the one who comes down out of heaven and gives life to the world'" (John 6:32, 33, cjb). Not only was He manna for those in the wilderness wandering for forty years, He is our bread today. Beth Moore in, *A Woman's Heart: God's Dwelling Place* writes: "The bread of God was devoid of leaven or yeast, just as the Bread of life was devoid of spot or blemish. He was the manna from heaven offered to all who partake of the Lord's table." He is our nourishment when the way gets tough—new every morning. He is our sustainer when we are weary.

Christ is the altar of incense. Incense speaks to us of intercession. Our intercessor to the Father is Christ Jesus. "He is totally able to deliver those who approach God through him; since he is alive forever and thus forever able to intercede on their behalf" (Hebrew 7:25, cjb). David asked the Lord to let his prayer go up to Him as incense. Even more so will our Savior's prayer, as our intercessor, go to the Father as incense, "a sweet smelling savor" for us!

Christ is the veil. His body was torn, beaten, and bruised that we might have access to the Father. "But he was wounded because of our crimes, crushed because of our sins; the disciplining that makes us whole fell on him, and by his bruises we are healed" (Isaiah 53:5, cjb). When the middle wall of partition or the veil was rent from top to bottom, all had access to the Father through Christ. Prior to the veil being rent in two, only the high priest could enter the most holy place behind the veil. The Bible tells us to come "boldly to the throne of grace," right into the very presence of God. "Therefore, let us confidently approach the throne from which God gives grace, so that we may receive mercy and find grace in our time of need" (Hebrews 4:16, cjb). Christ as our High Priest makes intercession for our sins to the Father. He is our altar, our incense, and rent veil into the holy of holies. Many surely did see Christ ascending up into heaven, and possibly there were a host of angels all around the Son of God as He ascended.

Christ is the mercy seat. Inside the mercy seat were the "tables of the covenant" or testimony, "Aaron's rod that budded," and the "golden pot that held manna." These were very significant to the children of Israel while they were in the wilderness. Thus, the contents of the mercy seat revealed and was a reminder of God's glory during the wilderness wonderings and later in the temple. Christ Jesus revealed God's glory when He walked among mankind as the law giver, the bread of Life, and our staff of life.

Christ is our scapegoat and goat of departure. "Aharon (Aaron) is to present the goat whose lot fell to *ADONAI* and offer it as a sin offering. But the goat whose lot fell to 'Az'azel (scapegoat or scape demon) is to be presented alive to *ADONAI* to be used for making atonement over it by sending it away into the desert for 'Az'azel" (Leviticus 16:9, 10, cjb). Jesus Christ was both the sacrificial goat and the goat that was used as the One that would be presented alive before the Lord. This can be understood in two ways: First, Christ, as our scapegoat, went into the wilderness to be tempted and as goat of departure came out of the wilderness in the power of the Spirit to fulfill His Father's purpose. Second, Christ as our scapegoat gave His life as a sacrifice; His death was atonement to God for our sins that we might have life. After His ressurection, He presented Himself alive before His Father as the goat of departure; and as a result we, as Christians, stand justified before our Father. God loved us so much that He sent His Son to die in our place that we may have life. "He entered the Holiest Place once and for all. And he entered not by means of the blood of goats and calves, but by means of his own blood, thus setting people free forever" (Hebrews 9:12, CJB). Hallelujah.

Christ is the altar of sacrifice. On the altar of sacrifice, were two horns. The animals were tied to the horns of the altar when they were sacrificed for the sins of the people. The horns were the power that held the sacrifice to the altar. The KJV calls it "the horn of my salvation." The CJB says, "The power that saves me" (See 2 Samuel 22:3). The altar was where the blood was shed. Christ is the horn of our salvation. He was secured to a tree by nails as a sacrificial lamb. Christ is the power that saves. No other name under heaven can save.

The following is His fulfillment of the new covenant, spoken of in Matthew 26:28 and 1 Corinthians 11:25:

Christ is the new covenant. "'Here, the days are coming,' says *ADONAI*, 'when I will make a new covenant with the house of Isra'el and with the house of Y'hudah. It will not be like the covenant I made with their fathers on the day I took them by their hand and brought them out of the land of Egypt; because they, for their part, violated my covenant, even though I, for my part, was a husband to them' says *ADONAI*. 'For this is the covenant I will make with the house of Isra'el after those days,' says *ADONAI*: 'I will put my *Torah* within them and write it on their hearts; I will be their God, and they will be my people'" (Jeremiah 31:30 (31)–32 (33), CJB). This prophecy is fulfilled through Jesus

Christ. The Jewish people will return to their homeland as prophesied and will acknowledge Jesus as their Messiah. (Read Ezekiel 34 and 36, either KJV or CJB) Gentile Christians, through Christ, are partakers of the new covenant blessings: regeneration, the forgiveness of sin, and the presence and ministry of the Holy Spirit.

Christ is God, He is the firstborn, He is the son of God, He is son of man, He is second man Adam, He is the Word made flesh, He is the Creator, He is our healer, He is the temple to enter for worship, He is the bridegroom, and He is the husband. He is everything we need. He is the cornerstone of our salvation. He is the cornerstone of Messiah's community. We are His bride, we are His earthly temple for Him to dwell in on Earth, we are the Word that many will read, we are kings and priests being prepared for the New Jerusalem, we are His children, we are His family.

The final of Christ's fulfillment, this side of glory, will be when the time of the Gentiles be fulfilled and He returns for His family. His family will join Him at the marriage supper of the lamb, and will be with Him when He returns riding a white horse to defeat the antichrist, and when He sets up the New Jerusalem. His children will be with Him for all eternity.

Also I have other sheep which are not from this pen
(dynasty or household, referring to the Gentiles)*: I
need to bring them, and they will hear my voice; and
there will be one flock,* (one family of God, Jews and
Gentiles as one) *one shepherd* (Christ Himself).

—John 10:16, CJB

14

Distinction Between Family and Temple: But Yet One

Family or Children of God

The family of God started in the beginning when God formed man in His image. "We also have a great *cohen* (priest) over God's household" (Hebrews 10:21, CJB). A household is made up of a family: brothers, sisters, mothers, and fathers. The family of God includes everyone who calls on the name of Jesus as Lord and Savior and has asked Him to forgive them of their sins. He is the only One who can justify our right into the family of God and as children of God. He accomplished that when He paid the ultimate price for our sins on the tree at Calvary. "For what one earns from sin is death; but eternal life is what one receives as a free gift from God, in union with the Messiah Yeshua, our Lord" (Romans 6:23, CJB). "Therefore, since we have now come to be considered righteous by means of his bloody sacrificial death, how much more will we be delivered through him from the anger of God's judgment" (Romans 5:9, cjb).

> All these people (the patriarchs of old) kept on trusting until they died, without receiving what had been promised. They had only seen it and welcomed it from a distance, while acknowledging that they were aliens and temporary residents on the earth. For people who speak this way make it clear that they are looking for a fatherland. Now if they were to keep recalling the one they left, they would have an opportunity to return; but as it is, they aspire to a better fatherland, a heavenly one. This is why God is not ashamed to be called their God, for he has prepared for them a city.
>
> Hebrews 11:13–16 (cjb)

They believed they were part of one big family. What has happened to the family of God today? Many are entangled with the Gentile world system just as they were during the Old Testament times. When God started His household through Adam and Eve, they were perfect and after their disobedience, still yet the family He started; and He was not going to abandon or forsake them.

From the foundation of the world and beyond He knew, He had an enemy that would try his best to rob Him of His family.

We have to come together as a family, a continuation of David's house, and allow Christ, our High Priest, to unify us as a family. As of now we are a family with so many belief systems. There is only one way to God; but yet many proclaim there are many ways to God. And we are spiritually warring against those individuals; and also against those who claim there is no God.[1]

"Two are better than one, in that their cooperative efforts yield this advantage: if one of them falls, the other will help his partner up – woe to him who is alone when he falls and has no one to help him up. Moreover, an attacker may defeat someone who is alone, but two can resist him; and a three-stranded cord is not easily broken" (Ecclesiastes

---

1   It is not the churches that are disrupting the world system, it is family members of God's kingdom, individuals in God's family, disrupting the world system and they are being persecuted. Too many church members feel safe within their four walls, but how strong are they outside of those four walls. However, in this day and time, people are not feeling safe inside the four walls. Why? Because the world does not care about those four walls, but they are concerned about a group of people who comes together to proclaim that Jesus Christ is Lord. That, my brothers and sisters, is family.

4:9, 10, 12, cjb). A nation that stands alone is in trouble when enemies come at them. A nation needs allies. Unity is power and coupled with the power of God, we can stand a much-stronger force coming against us. "And we know that we are of God, and the whole world lieth in wickedness" (1 John 5:19, cjb). The nation of Israel was strong when they were unified under God's commandments and the surrounding nations feared them.

I have no idea how God will bring His children, David's house, together. It may not happen on this side of glory; but I do know one thing for sure, we will all see each other on the other side of glory as God's family—His household. Paul's advice was the following for the family of God: "For brothers, you were called to be free. Only do not let that freedom become an excuse for allowing your old nature to have its way. Instead, serve one another in love. For the whole of the *Torah* (law) is summed up in this one sentence: 'Love your neighbor as yourself' but if you go on snapping at each other and tearing each other to pieces, watch out, or you will be destroyed by each other" Galatians 5:13–15, cjb). God help us.

There were difference of opinion over circumcision, eating the Lord's supper, between the Jews, slaves, and Gentiles, but they came together, and when they came together they turned their cities upside down with the Gospel.

It was not until persecution came heavy upon the Messianic communities that they begin to scatter and depend on each other. God is calling His children to be family—a family that has a message to those who are living in darkness. "Everyone who rests his trust on him will not be humiliated. That means that there is no difference between Jew and Gentile—*ADONI* is the same for everyone, rich toward everyone who calls on him, since everyone who calls on the name of *ADONAI* will be delivered. But how can they call on someone if they haven't trusted in him? And how can they trust in someone if they haven't heard about him? And how can they hear about someone if no one is proclaiming him?" (Romans 10:11–15, CJB) We are all one in Christ, as family let us proclaim Jesus Christ and Him crucified.

Temple

We will find out that the temple and the family collide, and we are built up into one. We are spiritual temples. Jesus Christ is the cornerstone of our temple, our body. In other words, He is the cornerstone of our salvation. He keeps us intact with God the Father. He is our foundation, our sure-footing. "On Christ the solid Rock I stand." "So then, you are no longer foreigners and strangers. On the contrary, you are fellow-citizens with God's people and members of God's family. You have been built on the foundation of the emissaries and the prophets, with the cornerstone being Yeshua the Messiah himself" (Ephesians 2:19, 20, CJB).

Paul tells the Colossians to "Remain deeply rooted in him; continue being *built up in him* and confirmed in your trust, the way you were taught, so that you overflow in thanksgiving" (Colossians 2:7, CJB). Paul also stated, "Or don't you know that your body is a temple for the *Ruach HaKodesh* (Holy Ghost) who lives inside you, whom you received from God? The fact is, you don't belong to yourselves; for you were bought at a price. So use your bodies to glorify God" (1 Corinthians 6:19, 20, CJB). Paul is speaking to us as individuals and as a body or community of believers.

We have established that Christ is our temple, and we are the temple of the Holy Ghost, which makes us one in Christ Jesus. Paul further states, "For in him, bodily, lives the fullness of all that God is. And it is in union with him that you have been made full—he is the head of every rule and authority" (Colossians 2:9, 10, CJB). We are distinctly His temple that Christ dwells in, and we are part of the family of God. Because we have become a part of the family of God, we, as a body of people, were made into a holy temple for Christ to dwell in. This temple is not made by man; it is His blood that was shed and our acceptance of Him as our Lord and Savior; we are made a part of His holy temple. We are placed in His temple as it pleases Him as well as in

His body as it pleases Him. In His temple, we are kings and priests and in His body we are made up of many parts. "For just as there are many parts that compose one body, but the parts don't all have the same function; so there are many of us, and in union with the Messiah we comprise one body, with each of us belonging to the others" (Romans 12:4, 5, CJB). As being a part of His body, we are family.

This absolutely is a great mystery. A man and woman become one when they marry; when one accepts Christ as their personal Savior, they are added to the body of Christ and becomes one with the remainder of the Body. "Therefore a man will leave his father and mother and remain with his wife, and the two will become one. There is profound truth hidden here, which I say concerns the Messiah and the Messianic Community" (Ephesians 5:31, 32, CJB). There is definitely a distinction between family and temple, but yet we are all made one in Christ Jesus. This truly is a mystery, a beautiful mystery that only the Son of God can build. We cannot create such a mystery but we sure are part of it: God's temple, His family.

For indeed the body is not one part but many.

—1 Corinthians 12:14, cjb

15

Distinction Between Congregation or Community and House, But Yet One

Congregation or Community

There are many different congregations all over the world who believe that Jesus Christ is Lord and have accepted Him personally as their Lord and Savior. My local church, where I am a member,is a part of the congregation or the Messianic community. It would not be Christ's community of believers if it was not a body of believers and who did not accept Christ as Lord. Christ includes all believers as part of the Messianic community even though they are scattered all over the world. In the various congregations, services are held differently. Some sing contemporary gospel music versus the old hymns, some sing both, some do not sing at all. Some congregations use instruments and some do not have any instruments. Some community of believers requires the women to have their head covered and some do not. Some require a certain dress code and some do not. But as long as the main focus is on Christ and Him crucified, and believe that He is their high priest and their law-maker, and He alone is their door to the kingdom of God, they are part of the Messianic community, the body of Christ.

"For it was by one Spirit that we were all immersed into one body, whether Jews or Gentiles, slaves or free; and we were all given the one Spirit to drink" (1 Corinthians 12:13, CJB). As the body of Christ, there are various gifts distributed to individuals by the Holy Ghost. "Now you together constitute the body of the Messiah, and individually you are parts of it. And God has placed in the Messianic Community first, emissaries; second, prophets; third, teachers; then those who work miracles; then those with gifts of healing; those with ability to help; those skilled in administration; and those who speak in various tongues" (1 Corinthians 12: 27, 28, CJB).

At the time of Christ, "A Roman city was the physical embodiment of a monolithic system. In Rome the Capitol dominated the Forum, and the Forum was surrounded by temples. On the public squares of every provincial town were temples and statues of the gods and deified emperors—idols." Among all of those temples and statues, there was only one Messianic community even though they were scattered from Jerusalem to Greece and surrounding areas. However, these temples or synagogues, were run by the Pharisees who did not believe that Jesus was the Son of God. "He came to his own homeland, yet his own people did not receive him. But to as many as did receive him, to those who put their trust in his person and power, he gave the right to become children of God" (John 1:11, 12, cjb).

The majority of those who did not receive Jesus were the religious leaders. But there is a reason why they did not. Paul expounded on the reason in Romans.

> For, brothers, I want you to understand this truth which God formerly concealed but has now revealed, so that you won't imagine you know more than you actually do. It is that stoniness, to a degree, has come upon Isra'el, until the Gentile world enters in its fullness, and that it is in this way that all Isra'el will be saved. As the *Tanakh* (Old Testament) says, 'Out of Tziyon (Zion) will come the Redeemer; he will turn away ungodliness from Ya'akov (Jacob) and this will be my covenant with them, when I take away their sins.
>
> Romans 11:25–27 (cjb)

The body of Christ had their differences but their belief was in the risen Messiah. As a whole, they were the Messianic community just as the whole of all God's children today. Just as the early communities of believers needed leaders to keep unity in the body, we too need them today. Christ placed leaders in the body of Christ to carry on His work after His departure. "Then he went up into the hill country and summoned to himself those he wanted, and they came to him. He appointed twelve to be with him, to be sent out to preach and to have authority to expel demons" (Mark 3:13–15, CJB).

Was this the beginning of what we call the "Church?" Absolutely not, this was a continuation of what the Jewish people were supposed to be doing for generations, but instead it had turned into a man-made place to take from and not to give out. Remember where the congregation came together it was called the tent of meeting, and it was where God's glory rested. When Jesus faced the money changers, His memory took Him back to the writings of Isaiah. "I will bring them to my holy mountain and make them joyful in my *house* of prayer; their burnt offerings and sacrifices will be accepted on my altar; for my *house* will be called a *house of prayer for all peoples*" (Isaiah 56:7, CJB). Why do I say that His memory took Him back to the Tanakh? Well, Jesus overturned tables and cried out, "He said to them, 'It has been written "My house will be called a house of prayer." But you are making it into a den of robbers'" (Matthew 21:13, CJB)!

They failed in their calling, but Jesus was going to pick up where they left off and ordain His disciples, twelve Jewish disciples, to carry on His work where the temple priesthood had failed. "He came to his own homeland, yet his own people did not receive him" (John 1:11, CJB). The temple leaders were the ones who caused dissention among Jesus's very own people. This house of prayer was to be the meeting place for His children, His community of believers—both Jews and Gentiles. Because of the sin that had crept in, He established the house of prayer on Himself—the Rock, the Second Man Adam; but, a continuation of His first born son, Israel.

Every congregation of believers has leaders who are to carry on the work of the Lord. After the destruction of Jerusalem, the children of God were heavily persecuted by Nero (his reign 54–68). "Before killing the Christians, Nero used them to amuse the people. Some were dressed in furs, to be killed by dogs. Others were crucified. Still others were set on fire early in the night, so that they might illuminate it."6

During Domitian's reign, he "enacted strict laws against Judaism, and insisted on the offering in even harsher terms. Since at that time the distinction between Jews and Christians was not clear in the minds of Roman authorities, imperial functionaries began persecuting any who followed *Jewish practices*. Thus began a new persecution, which seems to have been directed against both Jews and Christians."7 Why is this important to recall. It is because when Constantine came into power, he established Christianity as the primary religion. Persecution ceased and the community of believers began to squabble once again. Many facets cover the reasons why there was disunity, which we will not delve into; but it did lead to the Dark Ages where we can say that there were only remnants of true believers, both Jews and Gentiles until around the fifteenth century when men once again began calling on the name of the Lord.

The Dark Ages was long and strenuous just as it was during those four hundred years between the Old Testament and the New Testament times. Christ had to establish His house on Himself. He no longer trusted man to have any part of building His body or His house? His body was not going to be built by works but by His shed blood on the tree, nor His house built on the sand of times or men, but on the Rock—Himself. His house consisted of the apostles and prophets as the foundation for the continuation of His house that was started in the garden of Eden, but He is the chief cornerstone. Without the cornerstone, the house will fall regardless what it is built on.

House

Christ did not build His house on sand, He built it on Himself—Rock as the chief cornerstone. He needed a sure foundation—a bedrock foundation; a foundation that hell itself could not prevail against or overcome: Himself. And we are a part of that house.

We, as the family of God, are being built up into a spiritual house. "As you come to him, the living stone, rejected by people but chosen by God and precious to him, you yourselves, as living stones, are being built into a spiritual house to be *cohanim* (priests) set apart for God to offer spiritual sacrifices acceptable to him through Yeshua the Messiah" (1 Peter 2:5, cjb), We are priests in the house that Christ built. "To him, the one who loves us, who has freed us from our sins at the cost of his blood, who has caused us to be a kingdom, that is, *cohanim* (priests) for God, his Father—to him be the glory and the rulership forever and ever. Amen" (Revelation 1:5b, 6, cjb).

We will be on active duty as well in the New Jerusalem. "Blessed and holy is anyone who has a part in the first resurrection; over him the second death has no power. On the contrary, they will be *cohanim* (priests) of God and of the Messiah, and they will rule with him for the thousand years" (Revelation 20:6, cjb). Did you have any idea that you were priests and kings now in His house? We are, we may not wear the attire as those priests in the Old Testament and also of those in the temple in the New Testament, but our robe is the robe of righteousness.

The way that Christ built His house is an example we are to follow to build ourselves up unto Him. "So, everyone who hears these words of mine and acts on them will be like a sensible man who built his house on bedrock" (Matthew 7:24, CJB). When we receive and live His Word, we are built on Christ the foundation that only He Himself built. Thus, we too must live by faith, knowing we are a part of a house, David's dynasty, that will last forever. "Trusting is being confident of what we hope for, convinced about things we do not see. It was for this that Scripture attested the merit of the people of old" (Hebrews 11:1, CJB). Since we are a part of David's house, we must be as David: have our hearts fixed on Christ, the rock of our salvation: our foundation. "My heart is steadfast, God, steadfast. I will sing and make music. Awake, my glory! Awake, lyre and lute! I will awaken the dawn" (Psalm 57:8(7)–9(8), CJB).

We are the Lord's house if we hold on by faith to His Word. "Also, Moshe (Moses) was faithful in all God's house, as a servant giving witness to things God would divulge later. But the Messiah, as Son, was faithful over God's house. And we are that house of His, provided we hold firmly to the courage and confidence inspired by what we hope for" (Hebrews 3:5, 6, CJB). Did you notice the phrase, "Provided we hold firmly to the courage and confidence inspired by what we hope for." No, we cannot see the framework of the house with carnal eyes, but with spiritual eyes, we can. We are one body built up unto Christ Himself.

We have been given a gift from His bounty and placed in the house according to what pleases Him. "Furthermore, *he gave* some people as emissaries, some as prophets, some as proclaimers of the Good News, and some as shepherds and teachers. Their task is to equip God's people for the work of service that builds the body of the Messiah, until we all arrive at the unity implied by trusting and knowing the Son of God, at full manhood, at the standard of maturity set by the Messiah's perfection" (Ephesians 4:11–13, CJB).

His ways are not our ways. His thoughts are not our thoughts. As His house, He wants us to enjoy each other and please Him.

> Therefore, if you have any encouragement for me from your being in union with the Messiah, any comfort flowing from love, any fellowship with me in the Spirit, or any compassion and sympathy, then complete my joy by having a common purpose and a common love, by being one in heart and mind. Do nothing out of rivalry or vanity; but, in humility, regard each other as better than yourselves – look out for each other's interests and not just for your own. Let your attitude toward one another be governed by your being in union with the Messiah Yeshua.
>
> Philippians 2:1–5 (CJB)

We are family and we are all part of the same House—the house that Christ built. There is only one body, there is only one house—the house that Christ built. "There is one body and one Spirit, just as when you were called you were called to one hope. And there is one Lord, one trust, one immersion, and one God, the Father of all, who rules over all, works through all and is in all" (Ephesians 4:4–6, cjb).

Finally, am I admonishing you to quit using the word Church? No, I am not. The purpose for this book was to give to you what has been revealed to me. As long as we understand that Church includes all of God's children, the family of God, I truly don't think it matters if you use the word church. I do not expect a change that drastic come from me. I am a mere vessel of God to give what has been given to me. With the understanding that we are all a part of something wonderful, and I don't believe none of us will fully understand all of God's divine purpose until we are united with Him in glory. "Why, no one ever hated his own flesh! On the contrary, he feeds it well and takes care of it, just as the Messiah does the Messianic Community, because we are parts of his Body. ...There is profound truth (mystery kjv) hidden here, which I say concerns the Messiah and the Messianic Community" (Ephesians 5:29, 30, 32, cjb). My sole purpose for this book is to help you understand that all of His children are equal in God's eyes. Our focus must be on Jesus Christ and Him crucified, and taking advantage every time a door is open, telling others about His good news which includes salvation by faith and family.

Yes, there is a distinction between the community of believers and the house, but yet we are both in the same because we are part of the body of Christ being built up into a spiritual house: the house that Christ built. There is a definite distinction between the house that Christ built and all other entities that man has built.

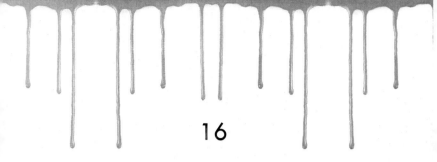

16

Distinction of the House That Christ the Messiah Built

A Banner

Every nation has a banner or flag that they rally around. The Old Testament states in Psalms 60:6(4), 7(5), CJB, "To those who fear you because of the truth you gave a banner to rally around, so that those you love could be rescued; so save with your right hand, and answer us!" In the Song of Solomon 2:4, CJB, says, "He brings me to the banquet hall; his banner over me is love." In addition, Isaiah 13:2 says, "Hoist a banner (flag) on a high mountain, shout to [the invaders]; beckon them to enter the Nobles' Gate."

The banner mentioned in Psalms 60 is referring to a flag on a flagpole; the second one mentioned is referring to: a *standard* over me is love. The primary root from both Psalms and Isaiah is to gleam from afar (i.e., to be conspicuous as a signal, or rather perhaps a demonstration through the idea of a flag as fluttering in the wind: to raise a beacon—lift up as an ensign, standard bearer).8

"Then we will shout for joy at your victory and fly our flags in the name of our God. May *ADONAI* fulfill all your requests" (Psalm 20:6(5), cjb). "You are as beautiful as Tirtzah (Tirzah), my love, as lovely as Yerushalayim (Jerusalem), but formidable as an army marching under banners" (Song of Solomon 6:4, cjb). The description of flags or banners is to flaunt (i.e., raise a flag; figuratively to be conspicuous—(set up, with) banners, chiefest).9

These banners distinguished God's people from all other nations. When they were being obedient to God, where their banner flew: nations recognized them as a people to fear. All nations heard about them. We see this when Rahab said to the two spies sent by Joshua. "We've heard how *ADONAI* dried up the water in the Sea of Suf (Red Sea) ahead of you, when you left Egypt; and what you did to the two kings of the Emori on the other side of the Yarden (Jordan), Sichon (Sihon) and 'Og, that you completely destroyed them. As soon as we heard it, our hearts failed us. Because of you, everyone is in a state of depression. For *ADONAI* your God – he is God in heaven above and on the earth below" (Joshua 2:10, 11, cjb).

In the New Testament, a banner was not mentioned, but Jesus stated what would distinguish His family from others. "I am giving you a new commandment: that you keep on loving each other. In the same way that I have loved you, you are also to keep loving each other. Everyone will know that you are my *talmidim* (disciples) by the fact that you have love for each other" (John 13:34, 35, CJB). Christ's banner over us is love. The only way the household or family of God will be distinguished from the world is by the love that is shown one toward another: words of truth and life.

In other words, there always has been a distinction between God's house and His household from the Jewish non-believers and the Gentile world system and that distinction is love. I am not saying to discard banners. Banners do represent what nations; states; cities; religious organizations; etc. stand for. But the distinction between the people of God and the world is love: the banner of love. Hoist your banner high.

Salvation vs. Works

"For God so loved the world that he gave his only and unique Son, so that everyone who trusts in him may have eternal life, instead of being utterly destroyed" (John 3:16, CJB). Jesus came to *seek and to save* those who are lost. The Bible tells us that "all have sinned and come short of the glory of God," but there is also a way of escape. The way of escape is believing that Jesus came to make you free from sin by repentance. Jesus told Nicodemus, a ruler of the Jews, "I tell you that unless a person is born again from above, he cannot see the Kingdom of God" (John 3:3, CJB). When we are born again by the Spirit of God, we are made free from sin. It simply means, "For what one earns from sin is death; but eternal life is what one receives as a free gift from God, in union with the Messiah Yeshua, our Lord" (Romans 6:23, CJB). This free gift comes by trusting in Jesus Christ alone for our salvation. In the Old Testament, blood was shed to cover sin. Even during Christ's time, sacrifices were still being made because of sin. Because of Adam's sin of disobedience all of mankind fell under the curse of sin.

Jesus came to do away with that curse of sin by shedding His blood on a cross. The shedding of Christ's blood and His death on the cross was His penalty for our sins. He took our penalty on Himself. Anyone can be forgiven of their sins when they believe that He died for them and they accept this free gift that He gives to every individual that believes. Ephesians 2:8, CJB says, "For you have been delivered by grace through trusting, and even this is not your accomplishment but God's gift. You were not delivered by your own actions; therefore no one should boast." Salvation is a free gift.

The Bible also says, "That if you acknowledge publicly with your mouth that Yeshua is Lord and trust in your heart that God raised him from the dead, you will be delivered"

(Romans 10:9, cjb). However, after we believe that we have been forgiven or delivered from sin then works is good. The Bible says, "Faith without works is dead."

Works prior to faith is just that works. Works without faith will not merit Jesus Christ. It is good to feed the poor, heal the sick, and give to the needy; this is good as a nonbeliever, but it is necessary as a believer in Christ. We are no longer our own; we have been bought with a price and that price was the shed blood of Jesus Christ. After accepting Jesus Christ as Savior, works are done for the glory of God.

Sanctification

It has been mentioned already that Jesus suffered without the gate for our sanctification. Sanctification also comes by faith. There is an initial cleansing of our sins and there is also a continual growing in grace. The Bible tells us we are cleansed from all sins. "But if we are walking in the light, as he is in the light, then we have fellowship with each other, and the blood of his Son Yeshua purifies us from all sin" (1 John 1:7, cjb). Also in verse 9, it states "If we acknowledge our sins, then, since he is trustworthy and just, he will forgive them and purify us from all wrongdoing."

It is a defining moment when the door is opened to have access to the throne of grace and receive something that was lost in the garden of Eden—a relationship with

God the Father. "How blessed is the man who perseveres through temptations! For after he has passed the test, he will receive as his crown the Life which God has promised to those who love him" (James 1:12, cjb).

The Lord teaches us to pray, "Lead us not into temptation; but deliver us from the evil one." He will not permit you to go through temptations, or the enticements of sin that you might not be able to resist in your present stage of growth. Use your temptations or tests as a proving ground that through Christ you can stand. You are never tested by God, but the enemy of your soul will tempt and test you; only through Christ, you will overcome.

Every day that you spend in the Word desiring to know more about Him, the more you will grow in grace. He actually tells us to grow up in Him. Therefore, there is a progressive sanctification, different from the instantaneous cleansing of our human nature from sin. "We will no longer be infants tossed about by the waves and blown along by every wind of teaching, at the mercy of people clever in devising ways to deceive. Instead, speaking the truth in love, we will in every respect grow up into him who is the head the Messiah. Under his control, the whole body is being fitted and held together by the support of every joint, with each part working to fulfill its function; this is how the body grows and builds itself up in love" (Ephesians 4:14–16, cjb). This is how the body of Christ will grow up in Him—each member growing up to full maturity in Him.

Baptism in the Holy Ghost

Another distinction in the house that Christ built is our relationship with the Holy Ghost. Many believe He was for the days of Acts. Others regard that today He is not that important to hear about. Nonetheless, Jesus told His disciples when He was about to leave that He had to go away in order for the Comforter to come and that He, the Comforter, would be with them and guide them into all truth. The key to knowing Him is to love Him and keep His commands. "If you love me, you will keep my commands, and I will ask the Father, and he will give you another comforting Counselor like me, the Spirit of Truth, to be with you forever. I have told you these things while I am still with you. But the Counselor, the *Ruach HaKodesh* (Holy Ghost), whom the Father will send in my name, will teach you everything: that is, he will remind you of everything I have said to you" (John 14:15, 16, 25, 26, cjb).

When Jesus was ascending up into heaven after His resurrection, He told those watching Him to go up to Jerusalem and tarry and wait for the Holy Ghost. Luke reminded Jesus's followers of this in Acts 1:4, 5 (cjb). "At one of these gatherings, he instructed them not to leave Yerushalayim but to 'wait for what the Father promised, which you heard about from me. For Yochanan (John) used to immerse people in water; but in a few days, you will be immersed in the *Ruach HaKodesh*!'" In order for anyone to be baptized in the Holy Ghost, He or she has to have a personal relationship with Jesus Christ by grace through faith. Understand that the Holy Ghost and the Spirit of God is the same.

Scripture tells us that understanding who Jesus is will be a revelation by the Holy Ghost. The Holy Ghost or Holy Spirit convicts a sinner of his or her sin and reveals to them they need a Savior who will forgive them of their sin. I am referring to the sin that all are born with because of Adam and Eve's disobedience of sin in the garden of Eden: missing the mark sin. Because of Adam and Eve's perfect human nature being corrupt, their human nature became full of sin. Thereafter, every one born is born with this sinful human nature. Only through Christ can an individual be forgiven of their sin and their human nature restored to a perfect human nature—to the very nature that Adam and Eve had prior to their disobedience. And now through Christ, a divine nature is imputed into one who has been forgiven of their sins. Does that mean we cannot sin? No, we can still choose to sin if tempted to sin, but if we do, we also have an advocate with the Father through Jesus Christ to forgive us of our sin and cleanse us of all unrighteousness.

But should we sin? No, we ought not sin and we do not have to sin if we continue walking in the Spirit, the Spirit of God (His Divine nature) that was given to us at our new birth. The Bible tells us plainly not to continue in sin in

Romans 7:24, 25, "What a miserable creature I am! Who will rescue me from this body bound for death? Thanks be to God, he will—through Yeshua the Messiah, our Lord! To sum up: with my mind, I am a slave of God's *Torah*; but with my old nature I am a slave of sin's '*torah* (sin's law).'" Chapter 8:1, 2 continues with, "Therefore, there is no longer any condemnation awaiting those who are in union with the Messiah Yeshua. Why? Because the *Torah* of the Spirit, which produces this life in union with Messiah Yeshua, has set me free from the '*torah*' of sin and death." We have been made free from sin and death, so why on earth would we want to continue in sin and call ourselves sinners. Is that an excuse for when you do or say something wrong? In verse 12 and 13 (cjb) the Scriptures say, "So then, brothers, we don't owe a thing to our old nature that would require us to live according to our old nature. For if you live according to your old nature, you will certainly die; but if, by the Spirit, you keep putting to death the practices of the body, you will live." That old nature or practices of the body is our human nature that we are all born with. No way around that until we are glorified.

Let us return to the baptism of the Holy Ghost. Acts 1: 8 (cjb) says, "But you will receive power when the *Ruach HaKodesh* comes upon you; you will be my witnesses both in Yerushalayim and in all Y'hudah and Shomron, indeed to the ends of the earth!" The Holy Ghost is given to His children for power from on high to have the boldness to present Jesus Christ and His entire Word which goes beyond just being saved. He gives you the power to witness on the streets, in the stores, in your neighborhood, wherever you go. There are many timid children of God, *who have not received power*, because they have not been baptized in the Holy Ghost. That does not make them any less of a child of God.

Jesus breathed on His disciples prior to His ascension and told them to receive the Holy Ghost. Was this when they were baptized in the Holy Ghost? No, this was when they received the Spirit of God within their being that every child of God receives when they give their lives to Christ. You have to receive that initial evidence that the Holy Ghost resides in you at conversion before being baptized in the Holy Ghost with the evidence of speaking in tongues. Do all speak with tongues? No they do not. I have seen the glory of the Lord on too many faces and they have never spoken in tongues. Just as salvation is a gift, so are tongues.

The baptism of the Holy Ghost also comes by faith. Those followers of Jesus believed when Jesus told them to go to Jerusalem and tarry until the Holy Ghost comes. Faith is the support of all things hoped for that comes from God. If one doesn't believe that the Holy Ghost is for them, they will never receive the baptism of the Holy Ghost, not realizing that He is in them at conversion. They just have not yielded everything over to Him, especially the most unruliest member of any body, the tongue.

Healing

Another distinction in the house that Christ built is healing in the atonement. Isaiah prophesied the following, "But he was wounded because of our crimes, crushed because of our sins; the disciplining that makes us whole fell on him, and by his bruises we are healed" (Isaiah 53:5, cjb). The kjv uses "And with his stripes we are healed." In other words, Jesus Christ the Messiah is still in the healing business. This too comes by faith and admittedly it sometimes comes by faith of the one doing the praying. Scripture says, "Is someone among you ill? He should call for the elders of the congregation. They will pray for him and rub olive oil on him in the name of the Lord. The prayer offered with trust will heal the one who is ill – the Lord will restore his health; and if he has committed sins, he will be forgiven" (James 5:14, 15, cjb).

When Jesus walked among men, He healed those who needed healing. When the Lord appointed seventy disciples and sent them out two by two to minister; He told them, "Whenever you come into a town where they make you welcome, eat what is put in front of you. Heal the sick there, and tell them, 'The kingdom of God is near you'" (Luke 10:8, 9, cjb). Jesus also expected His disciples to carry on in His name and have the same results.

I personally have seen the dead brought back to life. He has healed my children by the laying on of hands. He has healed me numerous times. Some have asked if sickness was from sin. The man that was blind from birth who Jesus restored his sight; the disciples wondered if it was because of sin. Jesus said, "His blindness is due neither to his sin nor to that of his parents; it happened so that God's power might be seen at work in him" (John 9:3, cjb). There are times sickness comes upon an individual because of their lifestyle. But whatever the reason, there is healing in the atonement. Because of His stripes He took, you can be healed.

"I am the 'A' and the 'Z'," says ADONAI,
God of heaven's armies, the One who is,
who was and who is coming.

—Revelation 1:8 (cjb)

Conclusion

I will end my book with a vision that God gave me a few years ago. The vision was this: "I saw a mountainous *wall* of *rippling* water. On top of that mountain of rippling water was a very large boat, just like we imagine according to Scripture what the ark looked like. Around me was a very large crowd and I cried out to those around me, 'Look, oh my God, Look.' Then when I looked up again, the boat was no longer there, but Jesus was standing on the top of the wall of water looking down at us with His arms in a downward position with His palms facing us. What He was looking at was people, just people looking up." I was not sure what that really meant until now as I am writing this book.

God's family was taken to safety by walls of water. And when the waters came together, enemies were destroyed. But once again God's people failed Him. Thus, He had an ark prepared for eight which were His family to carry them to safety from evil that surrounded them. After the ark settled back on ground, people failed Him again. The only solution was God sending His only begotten Son, second man Adam. He alone is our Wall of Water and our Ark of Safety. All who come unto Him, He will give rest. We are built up into Him; His house that He calls His own: we will find eternal rest in Him. Only in Him will we find rest—the Rock of Ages; the Rock that His household was built upon—Himself. I believe, in my vision, He was looking at His family and was just about ready to call them home unto Himself. Jesus said, "As for me, when I am lifted up from the earth, I will draw everyone to myself" (John 12:32, CJB). We are to lift nothing or no one up but Jesus Christ and Him crucified—no human being or movement.

"In my Father's house are many places to live. If there weren't, I would have told you, because I am going there to prepare a place for you" (John 14:2, CJB). He wants us to bring as many as we can with us. When the Ethiopian invited Philip to join him in his chariot, he was reading from the Tanakh. "He was like a sheep led to be slaughtered; like a lamb silent before the shearer, he does not open his mouth. He was humiliated and denied justice. Who will tell about his descendants, since his life has been taken from the earth" (Acts 8:32, 33, CJB). Just as God directed Philip to expound the Word to the eunuch, God is asking us to expound to others about Christ, His Word, and about His descendants: Abraham, Isaac, Jacob, Joseph, Esther, Deborah, Samuel, David, Solomon, and many others in His word—His family. We have to know the entire story of God. If we do not understand His descendants from the very beginning how can we explain anything about the house that Christ built—built specifically for His family.

> So then, you are no longer foreigners and strangers. On the contrary, you are fellow-citizens with God's people and members of God's family. You have been built on the foundation of the emissaries (apostles) and the prophets, with the cornerstone being Yeshua the Messiah himself. In union with him the whole building is held together, and it is growing into a holy temple in union with the Lord. Yes, in union with him, you yourselves are being built together into a spiritual dwelling-place for God.
>
> Ephesians 2:19–22 (cjb)

God has used many of His children down through the annals of history to make the path you and I am on brighter. I can name a few since 1903, but the whole story began "in the beginning God." God has always chosen someone to work through to bring change or to enhance the journey. If you look back over our history, there was, of course, Adam and Eve, Seth, Noah, Abraham, David, Josiah, Wesley, Luther, Bonhoeffer, Sunday, Tomlinson, Murray, just to name a few. Why He chose me to write this, I don't know unless it is a promise that is being fulfilled after forty years. On Tuesday afternoon, January 13, 1976, God audibly spoke to me, "You will lead My people." This was during the same breath that He told me that I would lose my children for a season and I did lose them that very day. I was holding my baby son of 4 months old and he was crying. Suddenly, I could not hear him crying but I heard God. Two of my three children were taken from me for 4 months, but God brought them back to me in a miraculous way. Therefore I know this was God speaking. No doubt. All of these years, I have wondered about that statement, when I was evangelizing in Africa, or teaching in Thailand, or traveling in the Mid-Atlantic region preaching, or when I was pastoring in Maryland. I quit wondering and just assumed it was all of the above. But now I am beginning to wonder again. Is it this book? We shall see.

What I am asking you to do, is if you believe what I have written, purchase one for someone else who has not fully accepted this truth or simply pass it on. We have to spread the word that, "For God so loved the world that he gave his only and unique Son, so that everyone who trusts in him may have eternal life, instead of being utterly destroyed" (John 3:16, cjb). That word "world" is referring to "orderly arrangement, adorning."10 We know the world, referring to cosmos, as a whole is not in utterly arrangement or is it adorning; it is full of chaos and darkness. The only thing that is in orderly arrangement and adorning is what God has created with His own hands through Christ Jesus—His house, His family. This word "world" is simply referring to the whole world of His own who trust in Him—His family. "Let us rejoice and be glad! Let us give him the glory! For the time has come for the wedding of the Lamb, and his Bride has prepared herself – fine linen, bright and clean has been given her to wear" (Revelation 19:7, 8, CJB). "Also I saw the holy city, New Yerushalayim, coming down out of heaven from God, prepared like a bride beautifully dressed (adorned) for her husband" (Revelation 21:2, CJB).

Christ gave everything to His bride that she needed to present herself to Him. Not one man-made thing is attached to her beauty, her adornment. Everything has been arranged in an orderly fashion for that gathering of His children, His bride who will consummate with Him at the meeting in the air—those who will attend the marriage supper of the Lamb. It absolutely all culminates into one: the body of the Lord Jesus Christ—His Temple, His house, His household. This is the house that Christ built for Himself to enjoy for all eternity, a world without end.

His work will be complete here on this earth. "All the fullness of God has been hidden in Christ, the Cornerstone, including God's infinite riches and immutable promises. As we live today in Jesus' name we rest in the fullness of His completion, for Paul said plainly, 'You also are complete through your union with Christ'" (Colossians 2:10).11 "As for husbands, love your wives, just as the Messiah loved the Messianic Community, indeed, gave himself up on its behalf, in order to set it apart for God, making it clean through immersion in the *mikveh* (bath or pool), so to speak, in order to present the Messianic Community to himself as a bride to be proud of, without a spot, wrinkle or any such thing, but holy and without defect" (Ephesians 5:25–27, CJB). All God's children: His household, His family will be caught up together when He comes for us and we will meet Him in the air and reign with Him. We will forever be with our Lord and Savior, Jesus Christ—King of kings and Lord of lords: Yeshua the Messiah. Hallelujah.

"Then I heard what sounded like the roar of a huge crowd, like the sound of rushing waters, like loud peals of thunder, saying,

> Halleluyah!
> *ADONAI*, *God of heaven's armies*, has begun his reign!
> "Let us rejoice and be glad!
> Let us give him the glory!
> For the time has come for the wedding of the Lamb,
> And His Bride has prepared herself –
> Fine linen, bright and clean
> Has been given her to wear."

("Fine linen" means the righteous deeds of God's people). The angel said to me, "Write: 'How blessed are those who have been invited to the wedding feast of the Lamb'" (Revelation 19:6–9a, CJB)! God's family – home.

Get ready, brothers and sisters, mothers, and fathers, He is soon coming for His bride.

Endnotes

Chapter 2

1. livingword@aggressivechristianity.net
2. Richard Anthony, *Christ's Ekklesia and the Church Compared* online.

Chapter 3

3. Scofield Study System, KJV, Oxford University Press, printed in Korea. 38.

Chapter 6

4. *Strong's Exhaustive Concordance.* #4682.

Chapter 9

5. Jack Hayford and Dick Eastman, *31 Days Meditating on the Majesty of Jesus* (Tyndale House Publishers, Inc., Carol Stream, IL, 1988, 2007)110.

6   Justo L. Gonzalez, *The Story of Christianity, Vol. 1* (San Francisco, Harper & Row, 1984) 35.

7   Ibid., 36.

Chapter 15

8. *Strong's Exhaustive Concordance of the Bible*, Hebrew and Chaldee Dictionary: #5263, #5264, #5251.

9. Ibid., #1713.

Conclusion

10. *The Strong's Exhaustive Concordance*. #2889.

11. Jack Hayford and Dick Eastman, *31 Days Meditating on the Majesty of Jesus* (Tyndale House Publishers, Inc., Carol Stream, IL, 1988, 2007)144.

12. Contact Dr. Grimmett for speaking engagements at arietta-grimmett@aol.com